Exploring Identity
and Belonging

Cornelsen

Schwerpunktthema Abitur Englisch – Exploring Identity and Belonging

von Anne Herlyn, Waldkirch / Sylvia Loh, Esslingen /
Birgit Ohmsieder, Berlin / Dr. Andreas Sedlatschek, Esslingen /
Michael Thürwächter, Heidelberg

Verlagsredaktion
Aryane Beaudoin, Dr. Marion Kiffe, Elke Lehmann (Projektleitung)

Layoutkonzept und technische Umsetzung
Ungermeyer, Berlin

Umschlaggestaltung
orangerie grafikdesign, Berlin

www.cornelsen.de
www.cornelsen.de/schwerpunktthema-englisch/

Die Webseiten Dritter, deren Internetadressen in diesem Lehrwerk
angegeben sind, wurden vor Drucklegung sorgfältig geprüft. Der Verlag
übernimmt keine Gewähr für die Aktualität und den Inhalt dieser Seiten
oder solcher, die mit ihnen verlinkt sind.

1. Auflage, 3. Druck 2023

Alle Drucke dieser Auflage sind inhaltlich unverändert und können im
Unterricht nebeneinander verwendet werden.

Druck: H. Heenemann, Berlin

ISBN 978-3-06-035492-4

PEFC zertifiziert
Dieses Produkt stammt aus nachhaltig
bewirtschafteten Wäldern und kontrollierten
Quellen.

www.pefc.de

PEFC/04-31-1156

Contents

Module III Crooked Letter, Crooked Letter   62

Abbreviations and symbols

adj	adjective	**p., pp.**	page, pages
f., ff.	and the following page(s)/	**pl**	plural
	line(s)	**sb.**	somebody
fml	formal	**sl**	slang
infml	informal	**sth.**	something
jdn., jdm.	*jemanden, jemandem*	**v**	verb
l., ll.	line, lines		
n	noun		

⊕ SPT354924-1 The webcode can be entered at *www.cornelsen.de/codes* to connect you directly to a website with additional material.

The Ambiguity of Belonging

Part A
Identity – exploring who we are

A1 Who are you? The puzzle of identity

1 On a piece of paper complete the sentence below in as many ways as possible.

> 'I am ...'

2 Choose a classmate you know well and exchange your sheets. Add aspects to your partner's list that you think are vital to their identity.

3 Read the quotes below. Get together in groups of four and take turns explaining them. Discuss which quote you agree with most.

A

'Identity cannot be found or fabricated but emerges from within when one has the courage to let go.'

Douglas Cooper

B

'I am NOT a product of my circumstances. I AM a product of my decisions.'

Stephen R. Cowey

C

'I'd rather be hated for who I am than loved for who I am not.' Kurt Cobain

D

'Life isn't about finding yourself. Life is about creating yourself.'

George Bernard Shaw

A2 Presenting yourself

Read the poem below.

I
am
me and you
more me
5 than you
never only me
I
am
a breathless
10 multitude
of selves
rippling
the water
(sylo 31)

1 Rephrase the poem in your own words to find out how the speaker sees him-/herself. Start like this:

It's a person who ...

2 Work in pairs. Compare your answers to task **1** and discuss which factors (e. g. family, friends, gender, culture) might determine this person's identity.

3 Write your own 'I am ...' poem.

4 Form groups of four and read out your poems to each other: what new or surprising things did you learn about each other?

A3 Defining identity

Read the info box below.

1 Arrange the ideas related to the concept of identity in a mind map.

> **Info Identity**
>
> We all think we know who we are. Our identity seems familiar to us – after all, we've been
> spending all our lives with ourselves, 24/7. However, the term *identity* is difficult to define.
> Generally, it is understood to be someone's sense of self. It is the sum of a person's
> character, beliefs, personality and physical appearance, including eccentricities and quirks.
> 5 You may e. g. describe yourself as an intelligent, athletic, honest male. Your identity
> influences the way you see yourself, what you believe, how you act and interact with
> others.
> People's identities are unique: nobody on earth is exactly like anybody else. We use
> the term *individuality* to refer to this fact. Personality can be described as the various
> 10 elements of a person's character that combine to make up their identity.
> Identity is not a static notion. It is rather dynamic, as we all are a different person
> today than we used to be as a child. Also, your identity does not develop in a vacuum,
> rather, it is negotiated with society around us, and depending on who we interact with
> we may even present a *different* image of our self. The groups we are a member of (e. g.
> 15 family, peer group, clique, social class) are the basis of our social identity and the source
> of our self-esteem. To increase our self-image, we tend to attribute a higher status to the
> groups we belong to (= in-groups) and a lower status to other groups (= out-groups). We
> may even discriminate against their members.
> When we encounter other individuals, we put them in groups: based on visual markers
> 20 (e. g. clothes, possessions, ethnic group) we ascribe cultural identities to them, thus
> dividing the world in 'them' and 'us'. This categorizing helps us orient ourselves, but it
> can also lead to stereotypes, prejudices and, eventually, racism.
> The construction and maintenance of our identity may be problematic. Tensions may arise
> between our self-image and the expectations of society. They may lead to an identity crisis,
> 25 and there may also be conflicts between how we see ourselves and how others see us.

2 a Use your mind map to prepare a two-minute talk about identity.

> **Language help**
> - create/develop/establish/forge your identity
> - maintain/preserve your identity
> - lose/change your identity
> - conceal/hide/protect your identity

b **Speaking** Work with a partner. Take turns giving your talks.
Compare your ideas.

A4 **What defines us?** *Beverly Tatum*

The following article presents the observations psychologist Beverly Tatum made when giving her students the same task you worked on in **A1**: 'I am …'

Which parts of our identity capture our attention first? While there are surely idiosyncratic responses to this question, a classroom exercise I regularly use with my psychology students reveals a telling pattern. I ask my students to complete the sentence, 'I am _____,' using
5 as many descriptors as they can think of in sixty seconds. All kinds of trait descriptions are used – *friendly, shy, assertive, intelligent, honest,* and so on – but over the years I have noticed something else. Students of color usually mention their racial or ethnic group. For instance: *I am Black, Puerto Rican, Korean American.* White students who have grown
10 up in strong ethnic enclaves occasionally mention being Irish or Italian. But in general, White students rarely mention being White. When I use this exercise in coeducational settings, I notice a similar pattern in terms of gender, religion, and sexuality. Women usually mention being female, while men don't usually mention their maleness. Jewish students often
15 say they are Jews, while mainline Protestants rarely mention their religious identification. A student who is comfortable revealing it publicly may mention being gay, lesbian, or bisexual. Though I know most of my students are heterosexual, it is very unusual for anyone to include their heterosexuality on their list.
20 Common across these examples is that in the areas where a person is a member of the dominant or advantaged social group, the category is usually not mentioned. That element of their identity is so taken for granted by them that it goes without comment. It is taken for granted by them because it is taken for granted by the dominant culture. […]
25 The parts of our identity that do capture our attention are those that other people notice, and that reflect back to us. The aspect of identity that is the target of others' attention, and subsequently of our own, often is that which sets us apart as exceptional or 'other' in their eyes.

From: 'The complexity of identity', in: Readings for diversity and social justice, *New York 2000*

1 capture sb.'s attention: make sb. interested in sth.
2 idiosyncratic: (here) individual
3 telling: showing what sth. is like
10 enclave [' – –]: area

Comprehension
1 Summarize Beverly Tatum's observations in three sentences.

Analysis
2 Compare Beverly Tatum's observations to your answers to **A1**, task **1**. Which of the aspects you mentioned identify you as a member of a dominant or minority group?
3 Re-read the last sentence (l. 26ff.) and discuss its positive and negative implications.

Part B
Belonging – feeling connected

B1 What is belonging?

1 a Look up the word *belonging* in different
dictionaries and copy the definitions.
b Compare the definitions: What do they have
in common? What is different?

2 `Speaking` Work in pairs. Take turns to explain
and discuss the following statements, using
your findings from **1**:

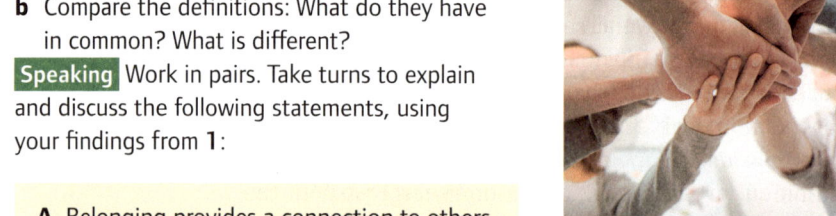

A Belonging provides a connection to others.

B Belonging is an essential human need.

C Belonging means you have to compromise.

3 Complete the following sentences on your own:

A A place where I belong is _____ because _____

_____

B A group where I belong is _____ because _____

_____

C For me, belonging is _____ because _____

_____

B2 What's the secret to happiness? *Mark Molloy*

1 Before reading the text on the next page, answer the question in the text's headline:

My secret to happiness:

_____

The pursuit of happiness can be a lifelong search for some – but researchers believe they may have found a key factor in feeling a greater
overall sense of wellbeing.

Individuals who feel a strong sense of belonging to social groups are
5 much happier people, according to new research by psychologists.

Nottingham Trent University researchers found that the more an
individual identified with a particular group, such as family, in their local
community or through a hobby, the happier they were with their life.

'Our findings suggest that thinking more about one's group life could
10 have significant benefits for an overall sense of wellbeing,' said Dr Juliet
Wakefield, a psychologist at Nottingham Trent University.

'We tend to identify with groups that share our values, interests and
life priorities, as well as those that support us in times of crisis, and we
can see how this would link to happiness. Our work taps into knowledge
15 that is deep within all of us, but which we often forget due to the
fast-paced and achievement-focused nature of modern life – that to be
your best self, you tend to require the support of others.'

They studied how 4,000 participants felt connected to certain
groups, and then measured the impact this had upon their levels of
20 happiness.

She added: 'It's important to note that identifying with a group isn't
the same as membership, though. You can be a member of a group with
which you feel no connection at all. It's that subjective sense of belonging that's crucial for happiness.

25 'Healthcare professionals should encourage people to join groups
that they are interested in, or which promote their values and ideals,
as well as advising people to maintain association with groups they
already belong to. Simple social interventions such as this could in turn
help to reduce NHS expenditure and prevent future ill health.'

30 Another study found that intelligent people could be more easily
distracted at work. So if you have trouble concentrating at work, it's
probably because of all those amazing ideas you have running through
your head.

From: The Telegraph, *23 May 2016*

14 tap into sth.: make use
of sth.
29 NHS (= National
Health Service): the British
public health service
29 expenditure: money
spent

Comprehension
2 List the factors that make people happy according to the text.

Analysis
3 Explain and discuss the following quotes from the text:
  a l.14 – l.17
  b l.21 – l.24

Beyond the text

4 Writing You are giving a speech at your graduation ceremony on
'What happiness and success mean to me'. Write this speech,
including information from the text above and the bar chart below.

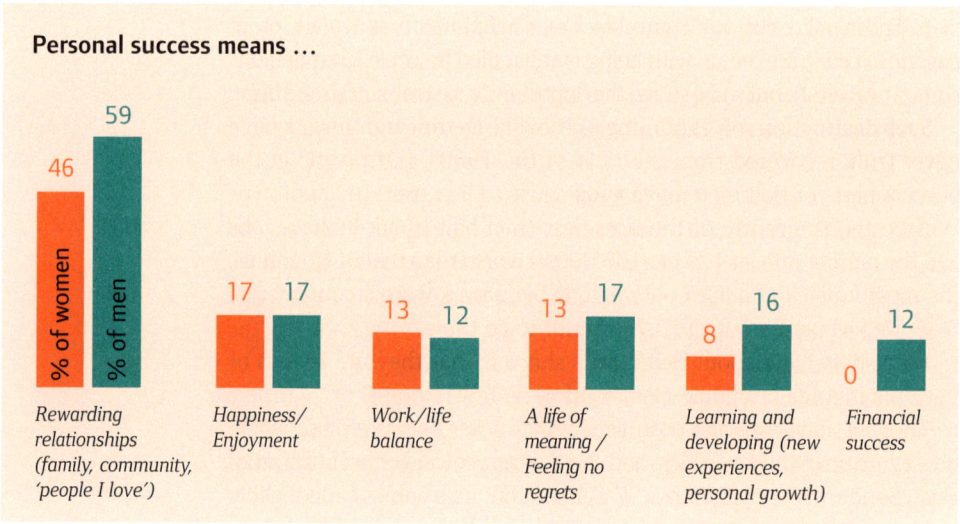

Personal success means ...

Survey conducted by Harvard Business School in 2014, based on 4000 interviews with senior executives

B3 Belonging to a community: Baltimore's inner city

1 The list below contains factors that could make a community vibrant
and livable.

a **Think:** Rank the factors from 'most important' to 'least important'.

Factor	Your ranking
A Tolerance and respect for people from different cultures, backgrounds and beliefs	_____
B Opportunities for cultural activities, leisure and sport	_____
C Co-operative and friendly behavior	_____
D Social inclusion and equal opportunities	_____
E Low crime rate	_____

b Speaking **Pair:** Work with a partner and discuss the factors.
Agree on a ranking.
c Speaking **Share:** In class, discuss the factors you did not agree on.

Fixing America's inner cities

As Baltimoreans sweep up broken glass and haggle with insurers over fire-gutted shops, many are wondering why the city exploded into riots last month, and how to stop it happening again. The proximate cause of the mayhem is clear: it erupted after Freddie Gray, an African-American
5 man, died in police custody. Young black men in Baltimore, as in many other American cities, are fed up with being manhandled by cops. Most demonstrated peacefully, but some seized the opportunity to steal, smash and burn.

Such destruction solves nothing – cities like Detroit and Newark have never truly recovered from the riots of the 1960s. But people in the
10 poorest parts of Baltimore have good cause to be upset. In Sandtown-Winchester, the centre of the riots, less than half of adults have jobs and the murder rate, at 129 per 100,000, is worse than that of Honduras, the most homicidal nation on Earth. If Sandtown were a country, the State Department would advise you not to go there.

15 What is striking about Baltimore's slums is that they are islands of dystopia in a sea of middle-class comfort. A few minutes' drive from a world-class university and posh waterfront oyster bars is a place where houses are practically worthless and shopkeepers cower behind bulletproof glass. Sandtown's population is 97% black, but its troubles cannot glibly
20 be blamed on white oppression. Baltimore has a black mayor, a black police chief and a black state's attorney, who swiftly indicted six police officers for the death of Mr Gray on charges including second-degree murder.

Black America's problems, like America's, are unevenly spread. Many African-Americans live white-picket-fence lives, but some cluster in
25 districts of utter dysfunction, especially in cities where old industries have vanished. According to the Economic Policy Institute, a left-leaning think-tank, 45% of poor African-American children live in areas where 30% or more of their neighbours are poor. Only 12% of poor white children live amid such concentrated poverty.

30 The causes of all this are complex. Some are historical: residential segregation by race was once the law in parts of America. Some are to do with family breakdown. Fifty years ago Daniel Patrick Moynihan, then an official in the Department of Labour, warned that the collapse of the black family was making black neighbourhoods poorer and more
35 violent. At the time, 25% of black babies were born to single mothers; now the figure is an astounding 71%. Boys who grow up without fathers do worse in school, earn less as adults and are more likely to fall foul of the law. And single-parent families find it harder to save money, which is one reason why the assets of black households are worth less than
40 those of white ones even when they earn as much (which most do not).

Growing up in a slum constricts your life chances. It is hard to learn in a school where doing your homework gets you ostracised, or to aspire to a good job when no one you know has one. For individuals the best answer may be to move. That is what much of the black middle class

1 haggle over sth. with sb.: argue with sb. about sth. to reach an agreement
2 fire-gutted: destroyed through fire
3 proximate: most probable
4 mayhem ['meɪhem]: confusion and fear
6 manhandle sb.: (esp. of police) handle sb. roughly
14 homicidal [ˌhɑːmɪ'saɪdl] (here) having a high rate of murders
21 glib: clever, but insincere
22 indict sb. [ɪn'daɪt]: charge sb. with a crime
23 second degree murder: *Totschlag*
27 vanish: disappear
39 asset: things that people own
42 ostracize sb.: refuse to meet or talk to sb.

Abandoned row house block in Baltimore

45 has done. And an experiment that allowed randomly selected families in very poor areas to move to nicer ones by giving them housing vouchers found that their children grew up to earn 31% more than peers who were left behind. However, the government cannot simply pay everyone who lives in a rough part of town to move out. It would 50 cost a fortune and be politically impossible. Rather, policymakers should try harder to expand opportunities for those who remain.

The two priorities should be safer streets – no one wants to open a business in a free-fire zone – and better-nurtured minds. Cutting crime means shrewder, less heavy-handed policing, so that locals co-operate 55 with cops. It means swift and certain punishments for criminals, but not necessarily harsh ones. An offender who stays out of prison wearing a GPS-enabled ankle bracelet is easier to track, reform and reintegrate into society. Legalising drugs would help too, since drug dollars empower gangsters and give them something to fight over.

60 The task of nurturing minds begins in the womb, with better prenatal health care. It then requires better nurseries and more school choice, so that parents can move their children out of chaotic classrooms and into more motivated ones.

The sheer ambition of this agenda is a measure of how deep-set the 65 slums' problems have become. But if policymakers want to stop America's inner cities exploding, they must pay more attention to the tensions building up inside them.

From: Fixing America's inner cities, The Economist, 19 May 2015

54 shrewd: clever
54 heavy-handed: using unnecessary force
55 swift: happening immediately
57 ankle-bracelet: *Fußfessel*
60 womb [wu:m]: *Gebärmutter*

Comprehension

2 Choose the correct answer. Indicate the line(s) and give a quote.

Baltimore saw an outbreak of violence …
- **A** after an African American policeman had been killed.
- **B** after an explosion had destroyed shops.
- **C** because African Americans had demonstrated illegally.
- **D** because an African American man died after being arrested by police.

line: _____ quote: _____

3 Choose the correct answer. Indicate the line(s) and give a quote.

> **The riots took place in a neighborhood …**
> **A** on the outskirts of Baltimore.
> **B** that has the highest youth unemployment in the USA.
> **C** with a murder rate that is among the highest worldwide.
> **D** that is predominantly Honduran.
>
> line: _____ quote: _____

4 Choose whether the following statement is true or false. Indicate the line(s) and give a quote.

> **Statement**   **True**   **False**
> The majority of African American people lead uncomfortable lives today.
>
> line: _____ quote: _____

5 Choose the correct answer. Indicate the line(s) and give a quote.

> **The main challenge faced by African American people living in slums is …**
> **A** institutional racism.
> **B** poor leadership.
> **C** widespread poverty.
> **D** white oppression.
>
> line: _____ quote: _____

6 Use information from the text to complete the following sentence:

> The structure of the modern African American family has changed in that _____
>
> _____

7 Choose the correct answer. Indicate the line(s) and give a quote.

> **Growing up Black in a slum limits children's chances in life because …**
> **A** children attend school irregularly.
> **B** learning is not valued highly.
> **C** schools have closed down.
> **D** teachers are the only role models.
>
> line: _____ quote: _____

8 The text makes several proposals on how to improve life in America's inner cities. Give three examples of what should be done and the hoped-for effects. Use keywords.

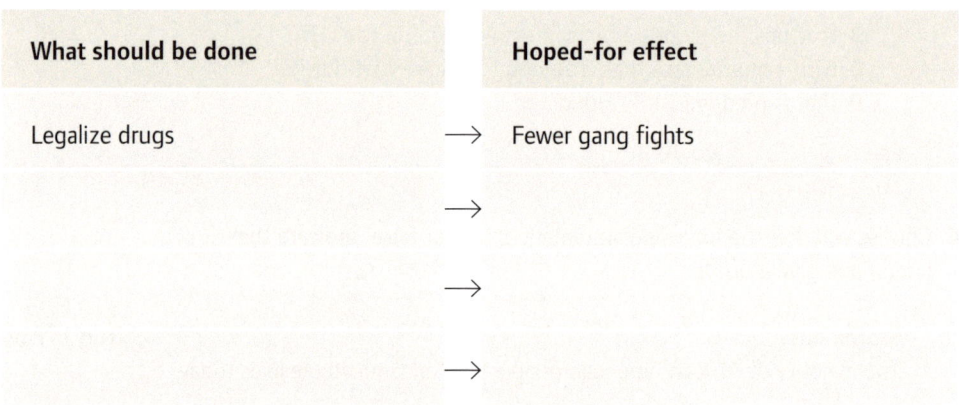

What should be done		Hoped-for effect
Legalize drugs	$\longrightarrow$	Fewer gang fights
	$\longrightarrow$	
	$\longrightarrow$	
	$\longrightarrow$	

9 Choose whether the following statement is true or false. Indicate the line(s) and give a quote.

Statement	True	False
The living conditions in America's inner cities can be improved easily.	○	○

line: _____ quote: _____

Analysis
10 Assess the strengths and weaknesses of the measures proposed by the writer to improve the situation in Baltimore.

Beyond the text
11 Speaking The Sandtown community committee wants to improve life in Sandtown. It has organized a panel discussion on the question: 'How can we improve our community so that residents take pride in it and feel a stronger attachment to it?' The following residents from Sandtown are participating:
– chairperson of the Sandtown community committee
– Black single mother
– police officer
– local shop owner
– teacher
– social worker

Split up in groups of six. Each group member takes one of the roles.
a Follow the instructions on the role card your teacher will give you and prepare the role play.
b Act out the role play.

B4 Defining belonging

1 Read the info box and create an acrostic
about belonging.

> **Info Acrostic**
> An acrostic consists of a series of lines
> whose first letters form a word when
> read from top to bottom.

————————————————————————————

————————————————————————————

————————————————————————————

————————————————————————————————————

————————————————————————————————————

————————————————————————————————————

————————————————————————————————————

————————————————————————————————————

————————————————————————————————————

————————————————————————————————————

> **Info Belonging**
> Belonging, in its most general sense, denotes 'being part of a group'. According to the
> US psychologist Abraham Maslow, the desire to belong is an essential human need: our
> longing for approval, acceptance and social attachment is one of the major driving forces
> behind our behavior.
> 5 Being part of a group can provide a feeling of connectedness. People that have a strong
> sense of belonging feel accepted and loved by others, which will shape their identity in a
> positive way by fostering their self-esteem and helping them create a strong sense of
> self. On the other hand, not belonging may have serious implications. If we are excluded
> from social interaction with others or constantly fail to establish social bonds, we may
> 10 suffer from loneliness, alienation, instability or other psychological problems.
> Gaining a sense of belonging may be achieved in different ways. Factors likely to impact
> our sense of belonging include our relationships with our family, friends and peers, our
> ethnicity, our social class, our gender, our sexuality and our age. But there are other factors
> determining our belonging as well, such as neighborhood, work, leisure, religion and nation.
> 15 Developing a sense of belonging is a complex process which involves a constant
> reshaping of our positions and relationships in society. As our circumstances change
> throughout our lives, this process never ends: belonging is best considered a journey
> rather than a destination.

2 Compare your acrostic with a partner.

Part C
Ambiguity – struggling to belong

C1 What makes belonging ambiguous?

1 Describe the cover of this reader and point out what it suggests about the nature of identity and belonging. → Language help

Language help
- rise to / respond to / take on challenges / face a challenge
- be/feel excluded/isolated
- experience/feel / suffer from loneliness / face discrimination
- be/remain undecided
- find/gain/win / long for acceptance
- be faced with / have/make a choice
- cope with conflicts/changes/challenges/struggles

2 Something is ambiguous if it can be understood in different, sometimes even contradictory ways. Explain what makes belonging ambiguous, completing the following sentences in as many ways as you can.

- 'Belonging to a group offers you … , but in order to belong you might have to give up …'
- 'We wish to belong because …, but might be afraid that this will …'
- 'Belonging to different groups may be a challenge because …'

C2 Struggling to belong: connecting to others

Edward Hopper: 'Nighthawks' (1942)

Info Edward Hopper (1882–1967)
Hopper was a prominent American artist whose paintings reflect his vision of life in the USA. His works often focus on the complex interaction of human beings with their environment and revolve around the themes of solitude, loneliness and resignation.
Among his most famous paintings are 'New York Corner' (1913), 'Automat' (1927), 'Hotel Room' (1931), 'Nighthawks' (1942), 'August in the City' (1945), 'Approaching a City' (1946), '7 a.m.' (1948), and 'New York Office' (1962).

1 Describe the painting above and analyse its atmosphere.
2 **Writing** Imagine you are one of the people in the painting. Write an interior monologue (→ Info box) from your character's point of view expressing your feelings at this moment.

Info Interior monologue
An interior monologue contains the thoughts and feelings of a character as they are passing through his/her mind. They need not follow a chronological order. Interior monologues are written from a first-person perspective.

3 What does the painting suggest about belonging?

C3 Struggling to belong: longing for acceptance

1 **Mediation** You want to participate in an international essay competition on the importance of belonging for young people in the 21st century. Write a 250-word essay about acceptance as a crucial factor for belonging. Include the main ideas of the text below.

Süchtig nach Anerkennung *Katrin Zeug*

Soziale Anerkennung wirkt wie eine Droge. Sie macht uns so glücklich, dass wir fast alles dafür tun. Kim Raisner trieb ihren Körper zum Äußersten, andere Menschen machen Überstunden, lügen, hungern oder lassen sich operieren. Menschen werden zu Gockeln, die mit Status-
5 symbolen beladen durchs Leben stolzieren, oder sie verlieren sich in fremden Ansprüchen, weil sie meinen, nur geliebt zu werden, wenn sie sich anpassen. Und auch Aggression kann ein Versuch sein, die Zustimmung zu erzwingen, die man glaubt zu verdienen. Die unbewussten Mechanismen treiben Menschen zu den unterschiedlichsten Taten, der tiefe Sinn da-
10 hinter ist aber immer derselbe: Wir wollen als Person wahrgenommen und bestätigt werden. Soziale Anerkennung ist ein Grundbedürfnis wie das nach Essen und Trinken, ohne sie kann kein Mensch existieren.

Kim Raisner at a press conference in Berlin (2015)

Und trotzdem geizen viele damit. Gerade hierzulande gilt das Motto: Lob ist, wenn niemand meckert. Skeptisch sein gilt als clever, Be-
15 geisterung schnell als naiv. Aber wo das Anerkennen fehlt, fühlen sich Menschen irgendwann unsichtbar. Sie werden nachlässig, unzufrieden, antriebslos oder gar krank. Nach Ansicht des Medizinsoziologen Johannes Siegrist entsteht emotionaler Stress vor allem dann, wenn es eine Kluft gibt zwischen großer Anstrengung und geringer Anerkennung.
20 Das größte Risiko für ein Burn-out ist demnach nicht die viele Arbeit, sondern das Gefühl, sich immerzu anzustrengen, ohne etwas dafür zu bekommen.

Wie weit Menschen für Anerkennung gehen und nach welcher Form sie suchen, ist unterschiedlich. Je nachdem welche Erfahrungen sie
25 gemacht haben, reagiert ihr Motivationssystem stark oder schwach auf dieselbe Bestätigung. Dem einen kann das Lob des Chefs Kraft geben, während der andere diesem misstraut und auf mehr Zuspruch wartet. […]

Nicht nur das Maß, auch die Art der Anerkennung, nach der wir
30 suchen, ist unterschiedlich. Viele Kinder, die vor allem für ihre Leistungen geschätzt werden, behalten diese Verknüpfung ihr ganzes Leben: Sie fühlen sich nur wertvoll, wenn sie Erfolg haben. Andere lernen, dass sie nur gemocht werden, wenn sie schön sind oder sich kümmern. „Je nachdem was wir erfahren haben, konzentrieren wir uns
35 bei der Suche nach Bestätigung oft auf einzelne Bereiche wie Karriere, Beziehungen oder Attraktivität", sagt Schütz.

2 Kim Raisner (born 1972): a retired modern pentathlete and current coach of the women's national modern pentathlon team

Doch wir sind dem Automatismus nicht hilflos ausgeliefert. „Den Menschen zeichnet aus, dass er die Möglichkeit hat, auch eine Außen-perspektive in seine Erwägungen einzubeziehen," erklärt Joachim
40 Bauer. Der dafür zuständige und evolutionsbiologisch junge Hirnbereich sitzt direkt hinter der Stirn und ist bei keinem anderen Wesen so aus-geprägt: „Der orbitofrontale Cortex speichert Informationen darüber, wie das, was wir tun, für andere sein könnte – eine Voraussetzung, um in einer Gruppe gut zu funktionieren, und unsere Chance, Informationen
45 zu prüfen und Entscheidungen abzuwägen." [...]

Ein Stück weit können Menschen sich also von dem Wunsch nach Anerkennung emanzipieren. „Ob wir zufrieden sind mit uns oder nicht, liegt weniger an objektiven Erfolgen als an unserer subjektiver Haltung," sagt Astrid Schütz. Und daran kann man arbeiten.

From: Die Zeit, 11 June 2013

C4 Struggling to belong: conflicting identities

1 Ndéla Faye, the author of the text below, calls herself a 'third culture kid'. What do you think she means by that?

Am I rootless, or am I free? *Ndéla Faye*
'No, but where are you really from?' It is the question that automatically makes the hairs on the back of my neck stand up. Like many 'third culture kids' (TCKs), I panic, wondering whether the question refers to my nationality, where I was born, where I am living now, or where my
5 parents live.

The term, coined by the American sociologist Ruth Hill Useem, refers to a child who has spent a significant part of their formative years outside their parents' culture. People who fit that bill have a tendency to mix and merge their birth culture with their adopted culture, creating
10 one of their own: a third culture.

Depending on the person and situation, I'll have different answers to that dreaded question. I'll tell white lies and change my story as I go, like many other TCKs. Sometimes I'll go for the quick answer: Finland and Senegal. Other times I'll tell the whole story: that I was born in
15 Helsinki, moved to Luxembourg, then to Brussels and finally to London. Or I might say that my mum is from Finland and dad from Senegal, but that I really feel like my home is in the UK now.

Each time I get the question, I feel like I need to explain myself, prove my origins, and because of that I'll often find myself omitting parts of
20 my story in order to make my identity more palatable for others.

Living like this can sometimes feel liberating: I feel as though I'm wearing different masks, and I am constantly able to reinvent myself. But this also presents a dilemma: who am I really? Which of these masks is the true me? Where do I belong? In my case, this is made even more

The flag of Finland and the flag of Senegal

6 coin sth.: invent a word
8 fit the bill: be what is needed in a certain situation
12 dread sth.: fear sth.
20 palatable: acceptable

21

25 complex as I'm biracial. Although I was born in Finland, I'm aware that
I don't look typically Finnish – but seeing as I've never lived in Senegal,
I feel strange saying I'm from there. Then again, I don't feel very Finnish
either, as I've lived abroad for most of my life. They're both countries
where I have family, and are places that I visit every few years – places
30 I think of with nostalgia. But when I'm actually there, I feel out of place,
like an outsider.

So where is home? Identity is attached to a sense of belonging, usually
through family ties or deep emotional connections. Home suggests an
emotional place – somewhere you truly belong, but I, like many other
35 TCKs, never quite feel at home anywhere. It feels sometimes that I am
in limbo. I am a strange mix of I-don't-know-what, and sometimes I feel
as if I'll never find that one place where I belong 100 %. I just feel blessed
to have had the privilege of experiencing so many cultures.

I sometimes wonder whether my life would be different if I had grown
40 up in one place. I wonder what it would be like to have lived in a house
where there were ruler marks beside a doorframe, documenting each
of my childhood growth spurts; to have a friend who's known me since
nursery; not to feel like a tourist, wandering around with a map in a
country that I'm supposed to embrace as my own.
45 Sometimes I resent the fact that I have to give complicated answers
to seemingly simple questions. At other times it all seems rather trivial:
as I watch my nieces and nephews growing up, and laying the basis of
their identities among multiple cultures, I cannot help but feel proud.
What an amazing opportunity, to speak multiple languages and see so
50 many countries.

Being rootless has given me a sense of freedom. I feel grateful for
the experiences I've had, and I am proud to feel, above all, like a citizen
of the world. The possibilities for the future are endless. The sense of
being at home anywhere, yet feeling that home is nowhere, is part of
55 who I am.

I love being able to choose to be whoever I want, wherever I go. My
many masks are a storyboard of all that I am. I've gradually built myself
an identity that is a collection of pieces, each of which I've handpicked;
choosing the best bits in order to create a whole. I've realised that those
60 pieces are not mutually exclusive, but that they are all dependent on
each other. Being rootless doesn't mean I don't belong to any one place;
it means I choose to belong to many.

From: The Guardian, *9 March 2016*

25 biracial: belonging to
two ethnic groups
26 seeing as: since,
because
36 limbo: situation in
which you are not certain
what to do next
42 growth spurt:
Wachstumsschub
57 storyboard: pictures
that show the outline of a
story of a film

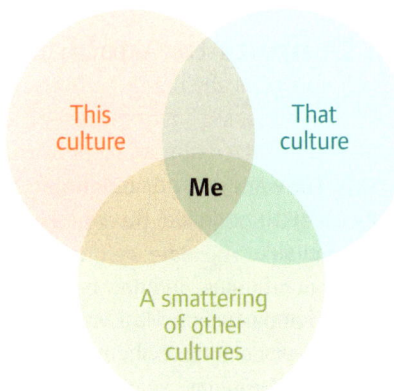

This
culture

That
culture

Me

A smattering
of other
cultures

Comprehension

2 Complete the following sentences using
information from the text:

A It's difficult for Ndéla to say where she is from because _____.

B A TCK is someone who _____.

C Ndéla has lived in _____.

D She feels most at home in _____.

E Her dilemma is that _____.

F Sometimes Ndéla feels out of place because _____.

G For her, *home* means _____.

H What makes her proud is _____.

I What is good about being a TCK is that _____.

Analysis

3 Point out the ambiguities in Ndéla's life and analyse her coping
strategies: how does she manage to deal with her 'dilemma' (l. 23)?

> **Language help**
> – *race*: a group of people sharing many similar physical features, such as skin, hair or eye color
> – *ethnicity*: a group of people sharing many similar physical, linguistic, social and/or
>   cultural features

Beyond the text

4 a Collect questions that you would like to ask Ndéla.
b Speaking Role-play an interview with Ndéla: one of you is the
interviewer, the other one takes the role of Ndéla and answers
the questions. Swap roles.

C5 Defining the ambiguity of belonging

Read the text.

Info The ambiguity of belonging

As we go through life, we are constantly changing, and so are the groups we are part of, our 'belongings'. The older we grow, the more independent we become from our family and childhood friends, and new people enter our lives as neighbors, colleagues, acquaintances, friends or partners for life. While being connected to others promises security, comfort and

5   happiness, being part of a group or community can also make us feel uncertain and insecure. We might, for example, be afraid of losing our individuality because we have had to deny some of our principles and conform to other people's wishes in order to belong. Sometimes the different facets of our own identity may be in conflict with each other, such as when we long to belong to different communities that do not share the same values.

10 Sometimes we might feel alienated or excluded, for example if we are not accepted by those we want to connect to because they do not have the same views or beliefs as we do. Or we might think that we simply cannot compare to the ones we wish to belong to, which may lead us to doubt ourselves.

The ambiguity of belonging describes the fact that there is no single or easy answer to the

15 question 'Where do I belong?' On the contrary, there may be many different, sometimes even contradictory answers to this question. Our need to belong changes over time in interaction with the changes happening in our lives, which may stir feelings of uncertainty within ourselves. There may be moments when we experience this uncertainty as a positive force: we are relieved we can let go of previous attachments and join new groups or

20 communities, which we hope will make us more content. At other times we may find it more difficult to deal with the ambiguity of belonging, for example if we are not sure about the solidarity and companionship of those around us. In moments like these, the search for our place in the world feels more like an ongoing struggle with no end, leaving us unhappy or even desperate.

25 Psychologists and social scientists claim that dealing with the ambiguity of belonging has become an epochal challenge in the 21st century. Due to the forces of globalization and technology, today's modern societies are characterized by increasing variety, diversity, and choice. While this has opened up countless new options and opportunities for people to meet up, interact and connect, many people feel that their lives are more complex today

30 than ever before, leaving them fearful about the decisions they have to make and possibly even disoriented, without a true sense of place or belonging.

1   Answer the following questions:
   a Why can belonging to a group make you feel insecure?
   b Why do people sometimes conform to other people's wishes?
   c Why can uncertainty be something positive in life?
   d Why does belonging pose a challenge in our society today?
2   Work with a partner. Compare and discuss your answers.

Part D
Me, you, us: exploring the ambiguity of belonging

D1 Looking back: what you have learned so far

1 Answer the questionnaire below.

> **Questionnaire**
> **a** How do you define yourself?
> **b** How do others define you?
> **c** How is your identity more than just the sum of the roles you play?
> **d** How important is belonging to you?
> **e** What makes you belong?
> **f** What do you have to do in order to belong?
> **g** Is there anything that makes it difficult for you to belong?
> **h** What happens to your sense of belonging if you find yourself in conflict with others?
> **i** What happens if you pretend to be someone you are not in order to belong to a group?
> **j** Do your friends and your family make it easy for you to be yourself?

2 **Writing** Imagine you were invited to contribute a blog post to the website 'The Belonging Project' (*www.thebelongingproject.org*). Write a post on the topic 'Why belonging is important to me'.

D2 Looking ahead: *Gran Torino* and *Crooked Letter, Crooked Letter*

While studying *Gran Torino* and *Crooked Letter, Crooked Letter*, collect information on the main characters (Walt, Thao and Sue in *Gran Torino*, Larry and Silas in *Crooked Letter, Crooked Letter*) so you can answer the questionnaire from **D1** for them afterwards.

Gran Torino

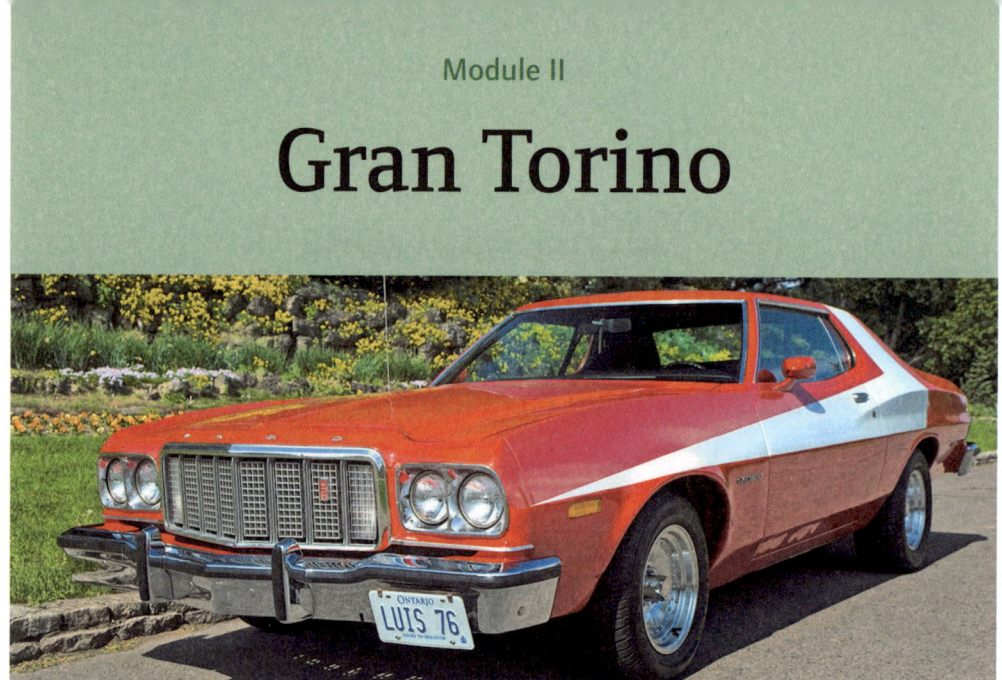

Part A
Information about the film

A1 Main characters

The Kowalskis

Walt Kowalski	retired Polish American assembly line worker; Korean War veteran
Mitch Kowalski	Walt's older son
Karen Kowalski	Mitch's wife
Steve Kowalski	Walt's younger son
Ashley Kowalski	Walt's granddaughter; Mitch and Karen's daughter
Josh Kowalski	Walt's grandson; Mitch and Karen's son

The Hmong

Thao Vang Lor	Walt's neighbor
Sue Lor	Thao's older sister
Fong/'Spider'	Thao's cousin; leader of the Hmong gang
Smokie	Spider's right-hand man
Trey	Sue's date/boyfriend
Vu Lor	Thao and Sue's mother
Chee Thao	Thao and Sue's grandmother
Kor Khue	Hmong shaman
Youa	Thao's love interest

Others

Father Janovich	Roman Catholic priest
Martin	Italian American barber; friend of Walt's
Tim Kennedy	boss at the construction site; friend of Walt's

A2 Scene index

Note: Different versions of the DVD have varying time designations.

Time	Characters/action
00:00:00–00:03:15	**Funeral service** The funeral service for Walt's wife Dorothy is held in a church. Walt seems angry about his granddaughter Ashley's appearance. His two sons Mitch and Steve, in turn, speak about their dad's unacceptable behavior during the ceremony.
00:03:16–00:07:45	**Confession** After the funeral service, Walt holds a gathering at his house. He is still frustrated and bad-tempered – especially towards his new neighbors, which he calls 'swamp rats', and towards Ashley, who is only interested in his 1972 vintage car and retro couch. Father Janovich tells Walt that he promised his wife to watch over him. Her greatest desire was that Walt goes to confession. Walt admits to the Father that his wife was the only reason he went to church.
00:07:46–00:08:55	**American cars** While all the guests are leaving, Walt fusses about Mitch's Japanese car. Having worked for Ford all his life, he cannot understand why they don't have an American car.
00:08:56–00:10:32	**New neighbors** Walt's new Hmong neighbors are holding a baptism ceremony. They speak about their teenage son Thao, who does a lot of the household chores.
00:10:33–00:11:21	**The elders** While Walt complains under his breath about not liking his new neighbors, their grandmother does the same about him.
00:11:21–00:12:08	**Father Janovich** Father Janovich comes by to see how Walt is doing. Walt, however, does not want to talk to him and tells him his honest opinion of him.

Time	Characters/action
00:12:09–00:14:52	**Two gangs** Thao is walking along the street and reading a book when teenagers in a car stop right next to him and start insulting him. Thao's cousin Fong and his gang pass by in another car and try to rescue him by insulting the first group. During the verbal fight, both gangs pull out guns. After the first gang leaves, Fong wants Thao to get in the car and join them, but Thao refuses.
00:14:52–00:17:20	**1972 Gran Torino** Thao and Fong meet again at Thao's house. Thao is doing gardening work. After talking to Thao's older sister Sue, Fong, nicknamed 'Spider', tries again to convince Thao to join their gang. He seems to be interested and asks what he would have to do to become a part of them. The others immediately start talking about Walt's 1972 Gran Torino.
00:17:21–00:19:49	**Life and death** Father Janovich finds Walt in a bar and insists on talking to him. When the topic of life and death comes up, Walt tells him about the three years he was a soldier in the Korean War and the horrible memories he will have in his mind for the rest of his life.
00:19:50–00:20:58	**Light in the garage** Walt wakes up in the middle of the night and hears someone in his garage. He charges his gun and goes to see. He finds Thao in the garage and pulls the gun on him. Thao trips on some tools, which, in turn, causes Walt to fall. Thao takes the opportunity to flee, running past Spider and his gang outside.
00:20:59–00:22:52	**Lions season tickets** The next day, Mitch calls Walt. When he asks him about his contact who has Lions season tickets, Walt gets mad, hangs up and goes outside to smoke and drink beer.
00:22:53–00:25:04	**'Get off my lawn!'** Thao and Sue are sitting on their porch when Fong and his friends pass by, wanting to give Thao a second chance at stealing the Gran Torino. When they try to force him, his family gets out of the house and they all get into a fight. All of a sudden, Walt is standing next to them with his gun and tells them to get off his lawn. Fong and his gang leave. The neighbors thank Walt and go back inside.

Time	Characters/action
00:25:05–00:29:17	**Hero in the neighborhood** The next day Walt finds people bringing flowers, food and gifts to his doorstep. He throws them away, but more keep coming. The family next door comes and thanks him again. Sue tells him that he is the hero of the neighborhood because he saved Thao. Thao apologizes for having tried to steal his car. Father Janovich comes by again and tries to persuade Walt to confess his sins and reach salvation.
00:29:18–00:30:00	**The barber shop** While having his hair cut, Walt and his barber Martin have fun insulting each other.
00:30:01–00:36:51	**Hmong people** Walt drives around and sees how Sue and her date Trey are being harassed by three African American teenagers. He stops and intervenes by pulling out his gun. Sue gets into his car. On their way home they start talking about the Hmong people. Even though Walt acts and speaks in a very prejudiced and racist way, Sue stays calm and tells him about the origins of the Hmong people and their culture.
00:36:52–00:38:37	**Horoscopes** Walt sits on his terrace with his dog Daisy and observes Thao helping a neighbor with her shopping bags.
00:38:38–00:40:34	**Retirement community** Mitch and Karen visit Walt on his birthday and try to show him the advantages of moving into a retirement community. Walt is insulted and kicks them out of his house.
00:40:35–00:47:31	**Shaman** Sue invites Walt to a barbecue at their house and he reluctantly agrees. When he notices that everyone behaves differently than he is used to, Sue explains the peculiarities of the Hmong culture to him. Walt then meets Kor Khue, who is a shaman and would like to read his soul. The shaman sees in Walt that people do not really respect him, that he himself is worried about his life, that he once made a big mistake he is not happy about, and that there is no real peace or happiness in his life. Walt starts coughing blood, goes upstairs and admits to himself that he feels more connected to the Hmong family than to his own. After that he enjoys his meal in the kitchen with all the Hmong ladies.

Time	Characters/action
00:47:32 – 00:51:31	**Youa** Sue takes Walt down to the basement where all the teenagers hang out. He gets to know a girl named Youa, who calls him funny. He then walks over to Thao, tells him that Youa likes him and points out that he doesn't do anything about it.
00:51:32 – 00:52:27	**Chicken dumplings** Hmong neighbors keep bringing gifts and food for Walt. He starts to accept them.
00:52:28 – 00:57:56	**Counting birds** Thao's mother has decided that he should work for Walt as a way to apologize to him. Since Walt maintains his own property very well, he cannot think of any useful work for Thao to do. In the end he tells him to fix the neighbors' roof, house and garden so that it can be nicer to look at.
00:57:57 – 00:58:51	**Coughing blood** Walt is coughing blood again and tells Thao to take his last day off.
00:58:52 – 00:59:48	**Dr. Chu** Walt goes to the doctor and is surprised by the new staff.
00:59:49 – 01:01:09	**Nothing pressing** Walt has the results of his medical tests in front of him when he calls Mitch. Mitch doesn't really have time to talk to him.
01:01:10 – 01:04:43	**Tools** Thao asks Walt for help with fixing his family's kitchen sink. They then go to the garage and talk about the Hmong gang as well as Thao's initiation of stealing the Gran Torino. Walt calls Thao a 'pussy' because he wants to hang out with these guys.
01:04:44 – 01:06:47	**Freezer** Walt asks Thao for his help because he wants to get rid of his old freezer.
01:06:48 – 01:07:52	**Good man** Walt talks to Sue while Thao is cleaning the Gran Torino. She says that Walt is a good man.

Time	Characters/action
01:07:53–01:10:24	**Past and future** Walt and Thao are in the garden. Walt tells Thao that he worked in the Ford factory for 50 years and Thao tells Walt that he wants to work in sales in the future. Walt advises him to go to school, get a job and go on a date with Youa, the latter with which he seems willing to help.
01:10:24–01:13:32	**'Son of a bitch'** Walt wants to teach Thao how to behave and speak like a 'real man'. They go to Martin's barber shop so that he can see how Walt and Martin talk to each other. They ask Thao to give it a try.
01:13:33–01:15:49	**Tim Kennedy** Walt and Thao drive to a construction site. Walt has a contact there and wants to help Thao get a job to earn extra money.
01:15:50–01:17:08	**Tool belt** Walt takes Thao to a hardware store and buys him tools and a tool belt for his new job. Thao is thankful for the help and support.
01:17:09–01:22:01	**Gang violence** When Thao is on his way home from work, Spider and his gang stop and assault him. They break some of his new tools and stub out a cigarette on his face. Walt sees what they have done to him and immediately wants to take revenge. Thao begs him not to do anything. Walt finds Smokie at the gang's house, kicks him in the face, pulls out his gun and tells him to stay away from Thao.
01:22:02–01:23:30	**The white devil** Walt, Thao, Sue and Youa are having a barbecue in the garden. Walt is in a very positive and happy mood. When he finds out that Thao finally asked Youa out on a date, he lets him borrow his Gran Torino.

Time	Characters/action
01:23:31–01:29:58	**Blood and tears** The Hmong gang drive by Sue and Thao's house and shoot at the house with automatic guns. Walt goes over to their house and sees that Thao is injured at the neck. They try to call Sue, but can't reach her. Shortly thereafter, she arrives at home with her face covered in blood. She was kidnapped and raped by the gang members. Walt is mad and goes to his house, where he starts punching cupboards. He sits down and becomes calm and sad. There are tears running down his face. Father Janovich comes over to Walt's house to talk about what just happened and what would be best to do. Walt seems more cooperative than in the beginning and lets Father Janovich call him Walt instead of Mr. Kowalski.
01:29:59–01:31:25	**Time to stay calm** Walt and Thao discuss how to deal with the difficult situation. While Thao would like to act immediately and kill all of the Hmong gang members, Walt wants him to stay calm and wants them to make a thought-out plan together.
01:31:26–01:32:45	**Let a man enjoy himself** Walt takes a bath and smokes in his house for the first time. Then he gets a new haircut and buys a fitted suit.
01:32:46–01:34:40	**At peace** Walt goes to church to make a confession. He tells Father Janovich about having kissed another woman in 1968, about not having paid taxes once and about not really having got to know his two sons. Father Janovich expected to hear something else, but absolves him of all his sins. Walt says that he is now at peace with himself.
01:34:41–01:38:08	**Silver Star** Walt takes Thao to the basement, tells him more about the people he has killed in the Korean War and gives him his Silver Star Medal. He then locks him in his basement to make sure that he doesn't get involved in the situation with the gang any further. He argues that Thao still has his whole life ahead of him.
01:38:09–01:39:29	**Police** At night Father Janovich waits with the police in front of Thao's house, fearing another attack. After nothing has happened for a few hours, they leave. Sue discovers Thao in Walt's basement and lets him out. He immediately runs out of the house.

Time	Characters/action
01:39:30–01:44:15	**Light** Walt goes to the house of the gang members and starts insulting them when they draw their weapons on him. Some of the neighbors hear their argument and start watching. Walt wants to smoke a cigarette and asks for a light. He starts to grab into his own jacket. Believing that Walt is pulling a gun, the gang members shoot him multiple times. After he falls to the ground, one can see that he didn't pull out a gun, but really did reach for a light in his jacket. Walt dies with his body laid out like a cross. Sue and Thao arrive at the location after the police. A Hmong police officer tells them what happened. He confirms that Walt was unarmed and that they have enough witnesses to send the gang members to prison for a long time.
01:44:16–01:45:08	**Life and death** Sue and Thao are dressed in traditional Hmong clothing and make their way into a taxi with their mother. Everyone is back at church for Walt's funeral. Father Janovich states that Walt taught him a lot about life and death.
01:45:09–01:45:59	**Gran Torino** A notary reads out Walt's will in front of his family. Thao is standing quietly in the corner. Walt is leaving his house to the church because his wife would have liked it. He is also leaving the 1972 Gran Torino to his friend Thao. Walt's family members seem quite disappointed.
01:46:00–01:46:20	**Driving away** Thao drives the Gran Torino, pensive.

Part B
Pre-viewing activities

B1 Working with a film poster

1 a Think: Look at the film poster from *Gran Torino* on the right and describe what kind of film you think it will be. Make notes on elements that influence your prediction. Such elements are:

the title of the film

the person/people on the poster

the images used on the poster

the colors and shading used

the font (style and size of the letters)

b Pair: Compare your predictions with a partner.
c Share: Team up. Discuss the following questions:
   – What do you think is happening in this particular scene?
   – What is helping you make this prediction (think of the different elements from task **a**).

B2 Imagining a scenario

1 Writing With your partner, write a short interior monologue (→ Info box 'Interior monologue', p. 19) for the character on the poster. Base it on your own ideas from **B1** task **1c**.

Part C
While-viewing activities

C1 Getting into the film

Making predictions

1 Describe the situation that is shown in the photo below. How do people act and what might they think during a situation like this one?

Comprehension

2 **Viewing** Watch the exposition of *Gran Torino* (0:00:00 – 00:17:20).
Pay special attention to the following questions:
- What characters are introduced?
- What are sources of conflict?

> **Info The exposition of a film**
> In films, as in drama, the opening sequence contains important information. The viewers are introduced to the setting, to the main characters and their relationships, to previous events that determine the plot of the film, and often also to the central conflict that the film will be dealing with. This opening sequence is called the exposition.

3 Work in pairs. One of you works on task **a** and the other on task **b**.

   a As you watch the segment, make notes on the following questions about Walt. Fill in the information in the table below.

What is Walt's full name? What does his last name tell us about his family's origin?	
What do you find out about his family? How is his relationship with them?	
What is his religion and his attitude towards it?	
What do you find out about his past?	
How does he live? What is his neighborhood like? What does he think about his neighborhood?	
How would you describe Walt's character?	
What does he value in life?	
What makes Walt struggle to belong?	

b As you watch the segment, make notes on the following questions about Thao. Fill the information in the table below.

What is Thao's family like? What is Thao's role in his family?

What does Thao's family think of him?

How would you describe Thao's character?

What is his relationship with his cousin and his gang? What is his attitude towards them?

How does he experience his neighborhood, especially Walt?

What makes Thao struggle to belong?

c Exchange your results with your partner.

Analysis

4 a Viewing A well-made film often works with contrasts and similarities. Watch the following scenes again closely and describe how this technique is used here:
- 00:07:46–00:08:05
- 00:10:33–00:11:21

b Discuss with a partner what these scenes show about the question of belonging.

c Write a short text in which you describe the contrasts and similarities in the two scenes and analyse their impact on the question of belonging. → Language help

> **Language help**
> while … · whereas … · in contrast to … · contrary to … · unlike … · both … · like … · have in common … · similar … · in the same way … · also … · thus …

Beyond the text

5 Work on **a** or **b**.

  a Writing Write a role biography from Walt's point of view (→ Info box 'Role biography'). Use the information you collected in task **3a**. Add his thoughts and opinions where appropriate. The following questions should be addressed:
  – What has shaped Walt's identity so far?
  – In what areas are his identity and his sense of belonging put into question?

> **Info Role biography**
> When writing a role biography, you are writing about one particular character's life.
> – Put yourself in the character's shoes and use the first person perspective.
> – Write like a diary. Talk about your family and your relationship to them, your everyday life, your neighborhood, your past, and your hopes for the future; tell your reader what is important to you and what causes you problems.
> – Write a text in complete sentences.

  b Writing After Spider and his gang have shown Thao the Gran Torino, he is left alone. What goes on in his mind? Write an interior monologue (→ Info box 'Writing an interior monologue', p. 19). Use information you collected in task **3b**. The following questions should be addressed:
  – What factors are shaping Thao's identity?
  – When and how is his sense of belonging challenged?

6 The film is set in 21st century USA. In order to better understand it, it is important to have some background knowledge.

  a Split into groups of four. Select one of the topics below.

A Detroit and its automotive industry	**B** The Gran Torino and American muscle cars

C The Korean War	**D** The Hmong and their culture	**E** The Hmong in the USA

F Polish immigration to the USA	**G** Youth gangs in Detroit

b Using the internet, find out about your group's topic and create a poster on which you present important information. Add images, timelines, etc.

c Speaking Present your poster to the class.

d Hang your posters on the classroom wall. They should stay there for reference while you continue dealing with the film.

C2 Belonging and not belonging

Making predictions

1 Work in pairs.

   a After you've worked on the exposition, talk about how the story might continue. Make predictions on what role the Gran Torino is going to play.

   b Join another pair. Present your ideas and discuss which of the suggested predictions is most likely.

   c Speaking Present your findings in class

2 Get together in groups of four. Look at the two stills and the quotes from the film (A–J) in the table below/on the next page. Using the stills and the quotes, predict how the story will continue and what kind of people are going to be part of the plot.

(00:24:50)

(01:18:40)

Quotations	Number	Speaker	Situation
A 'A brother to Spider is a brother to me.'			
B 'Get in the car!'			

Quotations	Number	Speaker	Situation
C *'Get off my lawn.'*			
D *'Just going to the corner spot, you know, get some CDs, sound good, bro? – He called you, bro!'*			
E *'Let me tell you something, boy. You step on this property again, you're done.'*			
F *'Oriental yummy? Oh don't worry, I'm gonna take real good care with her.'*			
G *'Those guys don't want to be your bros, I don't blame them.'*			
H *'What's the matter with you, for Christ sake? Trying to get yourself killed?'*			
I *'Why are you doing women's work?'*			
J *'Why didn't you call the police? […] Someone could have been killed.'*			

Comprehension

3 `Listening` Watch the segment from 00:12:08 to 00:36:51.

   a Put the quotations in chronological order in the table from task **2**.
Number them from 1–10 in the column provided.

   b For each of the quotations, make notes in the spaces provided in
the table on who the speaker is and what situation it occurs in.

   c Compare the storyline with the one you had predicted.

4 `Listening` Go back to the scene in which Spider and his gang try to
persuade Thao to join them for the first time (00:15:00–00:17:19).

   a List the reasons for joining a gang mentioned in this scene.

   b Describe Spider's character.

5 `Listening` Watch the final scene of the segment again (00:34:47–
00:36:51). Listen closely and fill in the gaps. There is more than one
word to each gap.

Walt: What's the matter with you, for Christ sake? Trying to get yourself killed?

I thought you Asian girls were **(A)**_____.

Hanging around in a neighborhood like that is the fast way to get you in the obituaries.

Sue: I know, I know. Take it easy.

Walt: And what about that goofball guy you were with. Is that a date or something?

Sue: Yeah, kind of. His name is Trey.

Walt: Yeah, well you shouldn't be hanging out with them. You should be hanging out with

(B)_____. The other Hummongs.

Sue: You mean, Hmong? Hmong, not Hummong.

Walt: Whatever. **(C)**_____, I mean Mong anyway?

Sue: Wow, you're so enlightened you know that? No, Hmong is not a place,

(D)_____. Hmong people come from

(E)_____.

Walt: Well how did you end up in my neighborhood then? Why didn't you stay there?

Two Hmong women in Sapa, Vietnam

Sue: It's a Vietnam thing.

We (**F**)_____.

And when the Americans quit, the communists

started killing all the Hmong. So we came

over here.

Walt: Yeah, well I don't know how you ended up in the Midwest. Snow on the ground six

months out of the year. What is it? (**G**)_____

wanted to be in the great frozen tundra?

Sue: Hill people. We are hill people. Not (**H**)_____.

BOO-ga, ga-Boo, BOO-ga!

Walt: Yeah, whatever …

Sue: Blame the Lutherans. They brought us over here.

Walt: Everybody blames the Lutherans. Well, you'd think the cold would keep all the idiots out.

Sue: (**I**)_____.

Walt: You know something kid, you are all right. But what about that dimwit brother of yours?

He a little slow or something?

Sue: Thao is actually really smart. He just doesn't know (**J**)_____.

Walt: Poor toad.

Sue: It is really common. Hmong girls over here fit in better. The girls (**K**)_____

_____ and the boys (**L**)_____.

Info Lutheranism
Lutheranism is a branch of Protestant Christianity. US Lutheran churches sponsored
many Hmong refugees after the Vietnam War, allowing them to resettle in the USA.

Analysis

6 Examine Walt's and Sue's attitude to the Hmong and to each other in the dialogue from task **5**. Look closely at the way they both talk about themselves and each other.

7 In this segment you are introduced to several young people who belong to different ethnic groups.

  a Make a list of the qualities and symbols the individual groups have to signify that someone belongs to those groups.

	Group: _____	Group: _____	Group: _____
Qualities			
Symbols			

  b List situations in the film in which an individual clearly does not belong to a group and explain how this is noticeable.

Beyond the text

8 Writing Imagine that you are Trey at the end of the day in which he and Sue get harassed by a group of Black teenagers (00:30:00–00:34:46). Write Sue an email explaining what went through your head during that moment, and commenting on why you felt helpless and felt like you didn't belong.

C3 Belonging in gangs to form an identity?

1 `Mediation` You have been emailing your tandem partner in California about why young people join gangs. Your tandem partner came across the article below and needs help understanding it. Read the article and write an email to your tandem partner in which you summarize in English why Hakan wanted to be in a gang.

Leben in einer Kreuzberger Türkengang *Matern Boeselager*
Kind von Immigranten, Gangmitglied, jüngster Bankräuber Deutschlands:
Wir haben uns mit dem ehemaligen „36 Boy" Killa Hakan über seine
Vergangenheit unterhalten.

In Berlin sind die 36 Boys Legende. Die Gang bestand hauptsächlich
5 aus den Kindern türkischer Gastarbeiter und hatte ihr Revier um das
Kottbusser Tor und die Naunynstraße. In den 80ern sorgte ihr Name
regelmäßig für Schnappatmung bei Berliner Innenpolitikern, Polizeichefs
und *Spiegel*-Reportern. [...]

Hakan Durmuş, auch „Killa Hakan" genannt, war von Anfang an
10 dabei. Wenn man wissen will, wie es sich wirklich anfühlt, als Mitglied
einer Kreuzberger Türkengang aufzuwachsen, gibt es also kaum einen
besseren Gesprächspartner—schließlich lebt Hakan immer noch in der
Naunynstraße. [...] Ich habe mich mit ihm über seine Kindheit im
Berliner Gastarbeitermilieu, Massenschlägereien zwischen Türkengangs
15 und über Möchtegern-36er wie Deso Dogg und Tim Raue unterhalten.
VICE: Hakan, warum heißt du eigentlich Killa?
Killa Hakan: Na, weil ich immer korrekt war. Wenn was schön war, hat
man früher gesagt: „Mann, Killa Auto, Killa Mädchen." Killa Hakan!
Bist du in Kreuzberg geboren?
20 Ich bin Ur-Kreuzberger. Geboren im Urbankrankenhaus, von da bin ich
sofort in die Naunynstraße gekommen. Besser geht's nicht mehr.
Wie sah die Gegend hier damals aus?
Das war dunkel hier. Das war ja hier direkt an der Mauer. Keiner wollte
hier was mieten. Nur die Kanaken sollten dahin, die machen das schon.
25 Und wir haben das gemacht!
Wie war das, damals hier als Kind von Gastarbeitern aufzuwachsen?
Wir sind jedes Jahr in die Türkei gefahren. Also, wir waren hier in der
Schule und so, aber wir wussten von den Eltern, wenn wir genug Geld
für ein Haus haben, dann gehen wir zurück in die Türkei. Mit dem
30 Gedanken sind wir aufgewachsen, jeder von uns.

Die wollten auch wirklich gehen, aber dann kam '82 der Putsch. Da
haben die in der Türkei gefragt: „Bist du links oder rechts?" Wenn du
falsch geantwortet hast, warst du weg. Also haben die Eltern gesagt:
Wir lassen unsere Kinder in Europa. Wer will schon seine Kinder ver-
35 lieren? Also mussten wir plötzlich alle umdenken, da mussten wir uns
schon hart umstellen. [...]

Wie hat das mit der Gang angefangen?

Da muss ich 12, 13 gewesen sein. Wie gesagt, als der Putsch kam, da wussten wir erstmal alle nicht, was tun. Wir waren sauer. Wir hatten
40 nicht mal deutsche Freunde—was sollen wir mit denen, wir gehen ja sowieso wieder, dachten wir vorher.

Aber in die Diskos wollten wir natürlich. Nur: Wir sind ja Moslems, wir hatten das nicht gelernt. Und wir sind natürlich nicht reingelassen worden—wer will schon sechs, sieben Kanaken reinlassen? Immer gab
45 es Stress, immer gab es Scheiße. Da haben wir gesagt: „OK, ihr lasst uns nicht rein? Wir kommen aber rein." So kam dann die Gang.

Was habt ihr dann gemacht?

Erstmal: Kotti sichern. Erstmal klarmachen, das hier ist unseres. Wir wollten, dass uns da, wo wir wohnen, jeder akzeptiert. Durch die Gang
50 warst du halt nicht mehr alleine, da waren dann noch vier andere, die waren genau so wie du. Dann kommt es auch nicht mehr so hart, wenn jemand „dreckige Kanaken" sagt. Dann macht dich das stark, das hört sich dann ganz anders an. So hat das ganz früher angefangen, die 36 Boys.

From: 'Mit dem Baseballschläger gegen Nazis: Aufwachsen in einer Berliner Türkengang',
Vice Online, 5 May 2015

Analysis

2 Work in pairs. One of you works on task **a** and the other works on task **b**. When you are finished, do task **c** together.

  a Compare Spider with Hakan. Consider the aspects in Spider's life that are not shown, such as his life as a child (→ Language help, p. 38).

  b Compare Hakan with Sue, especially their situations and attitudes. (→ Language help, p. 38)

  c Compare your results. Discuss whether Hakan's situation is more similar to Spider's or to Sue's.

Beyond the text

3 Split the class into four groups. Each group works on a different character: Thao, Sue, Spider or Walt.

  a In your groups, prepare to play the role of your character. Prepare to introduce yourself to the others, to share your opinion on gangs and to answer questions about your opinion. Gather all the information available on that character.

  b Prepare questions to ask the other three characters (→ Language help).

Language help

What did you feel when … ? · Why did you …? · What do you think of … ? · Do you regret … ? · Are you proud of … ? · Explain … · Would you …? · How do you feel about … ?

c **Speaking** Form new groups of four. Each group needs to contain one student from each of the original groups. As your character, introduce yourself to the group. Then the other group members ask you the questions they prepared.

d **Speaking** Remain in character and discuss the following question with the new group: 'Gangs – a surrogate for families?'

C4 A shifting sense of belonging

Making predictions

1 Take seven large sheets of paper. Write one of the following topics in the middle of each sheet and place them on different tables in the classroom.

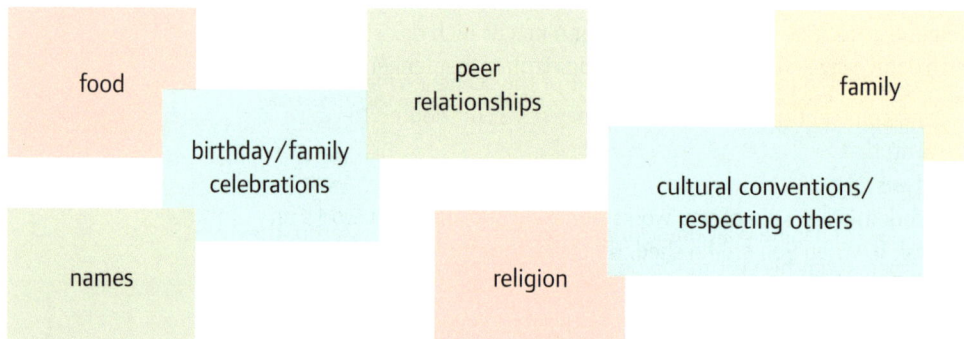

food

peer relationships

family

birthday/family celebrations

cultural conventions/ respecting others

names

religion

a Now walk around in the room and stop at different tables. Write down what the topic means to you. Consider how it shapes your identity and/or influences your sense of belonging.

b Notice what the others have written and add your own thoughts if you wish. Do not talk.

2 Split into seven groups. Each group is assigned one of the topics from task **1**.

a Read the comments on your poster and discuss them in your group.

b **Speaking** Summarize your findings in no more than three sentences and present them to the class, speaking in the name of the group, i. e. 'To many of us, family means …', 'Food is to us …', etc.

c How do you think these topics will be further developed in the film? Discuss with the class.

Comprehension

3 Viewing Continue watching the film (00:36:52–00:52:34).

a Keep working in your groups and make notes on what happens in relation to the topic you worked on in task **2**.

b Discuss your results in your group.

c Speaking Present your results to the class.

Analysis

4 a In your groups, discuss how the information you found affects the characters' sense of belonging.

b Speaking Present your results to the class.

5 Writing Write a blog post on the following quote from Walt in the film:

> *'I have more in common with these gooks than I have with my own spoiled-rotten family.'*

Explain the quotation in the context of the scene in which it is said and comment on it. What factors may have contributed to Walt's attitude?

Beyond the text

6 Writing Imagine Walt goes for another haircut. He tells Martin, the barber, about his visit to the neighbors' house on his birthday. He becomes thoughtful and starts reflecting on his sense of belonging. Write this scene. It should primarily be a monologue by Walt, but Martin may throw in a few words here or there.

C5 Male worlds in *Gran Torino*

Making predictions

Before watching the next segment of the film, read the following info box about stereotypes.

Info Stereotypes

A stereotype is a fixed and often overly generalized belief one has about a particular group of people regarding their gender, ethnicity, class, sexual identity, etc. The negative consequences of stereotypes are clear – they lead to prejudice against and discrimination of certain groups. At the same time, they can help create a strong sense of belonging to a certain group that sets itself off from another ('us' versus 'them'). For example, most societies have clear ideas of how women and men should behave. Fitting into a group that is defined by rituals of masculinity or femininity can create a strong sense of identity.

1 a Consider the still from the movie on the right. How does it reflect typical gender roles?

b Think of the way women and men are portrayed in *Gran Torino*. How are they expected to behave and who has these expectations?

c Work in pairs and fill in the table below with examples of gender roles and expectations from the movie.

01:16:42

Gender roles and expectations in *Gran Torino*: men	Gender roles and expectations in *Gran Torino*: women

d **Speaking** Present your examples to the class.

e Discuss the following with your classmates:
   - Find examples of gender stereotypes in your own society.
   - Name examples of behaviors that contradict these stereotypes.
   - How might the topic of gender stereotypes be addressed in the rest of the movie? Refer back to the still in task **a** when making your prediction.

Comprehension

2 **Listening** Watch the next segment of the film (00:52:35–01:29:58) and answer the following questions:

a Why is it important for Thao's family that he does some work for Walt?

b What kind of jobs does Thao do for Walt?

c What is the most probable cause why Walt calls his son Mitch?

d What is the reason Walt gives Thao for selling him his old freezer at a cheaper price?

e What helps Mr Kennedy decide to give Thao a job?

3 **Listening** Before watching again, take a look at sentences a–f
below. Then go back to the scene in which Walt and Thao are in the
garden, speaking about work (01:07:53-01:10:23). While you watch,
complete the following sentences by ticking the correct answer. There
is only one possible answer per sentence beginning.

a The Hmong consider this to be women's work:

  ○ **A** watching birds.
  ○ **B** preparing food.
  ○ **C** cleaning the house.
  ○ **D** taking care of the garden.

b Thao thinks that Walt should quit …

  ○ **A** smoking.
  ○ **B** gardening.
  ○ **C** being in a gang.
  ○ **D** making fun of him.

c Walt's lighter has a symbol that represents …

  ○ **A** the fifties.
  ○ **B** his very first car.
  ○ **C** his time in the army.
  ○ **D** one of his favorite bands.

d Walt used to install these on Gran Torinos:

  ○ **A** the gearing wheel.
  ○ **B** the steering wheel.
  ○ **C** the gearing column.
  ○ **D** the steering column.

e Thao is not optimistic about going to university because it …

  ○ **A** is expensive.
  ○ **B** would cost him his time.
  ○ **C** is not needed to work in sales.
  ○ **D** would force him to leave his family.

f Walt thinks that Thao could get a job in construction because he knows …

    A that Youa would like it.
    B it would make him a man.
    C people who work in that field.
    D how people succeed in that field.

Analysis

4 a Examine how the men in this segment behave. Pay special attention to:
- Walt
- Thao
- Martin
- Tim Kennedy
- the members of the Hmong gang.

b After having examined the men's behavior, answer the following questions:
- How do they talk?
- What are their ideas of suitable work?
- How do they treat others?
- How do they deal with conflict?

c Compare and discuss your answers in class.

d Compare the men's behavior in the film to the way men act in your society. Do they act a certain way to belong?

C6 Portraying the Hmong in *Gran Torino*

In an interview for an academic journal dedicated to Hmong studies, Bee Vang, who plays Thao in *Gran Torino*, talks about how Thao is presented in the film and about concepts of manhood in Hmong culture. Read the following excerpt from this interview.

An interview with Bee Van *Louisa Schein*

_____ *LS: So you were uneasy about the lines and character descriptions. Why did you audition and ultimately take the part?*
BV: Friends kept pushing me to try out. I didn't take it seriously. Didn't think I'd get the part. But when I was called back for another round of
5 auditioning, I realized I wanted to be part of the hype, because this would become a great cultural event of our time, especially for Hmong. Most importantly, my intentions were, as I continued to audition and do my best, to try to improve on the script and the ways Hmong were portrayed. I wanted to create a character that people could love. I decided

Vietnamese Hmong women

2 audition [ɔːˈdɪʃn] (v): give a short performance when applying for a role in a film
2 ultimately: finally

10 to commit to developing the role of Thao, making him more complex and
credible. I imagined a guy who would chafe at his subordination more. So
even when he had to obey, he did it with more attitude.

_____ *LS: Did you feel you succeeded in creating this character?*
BV: I added a lot of intonation and gestures to try to give Thao some
15 dignity. For instance, when my sister is offering me to work for Walt, I
raised my voice to a shout to indicate I hated the idea of slaving for
Walt. That outburst wasn't in the script. But most of the script was not
very open to interpretation and it was premised on his not having any
dignity. He needs to be clueless and have no self-respect in order for
20 the white elder man to achieve his savior role. He has to hang his head
and absorb abuse. So it makes me wonder how a character like Thao
could bring any change to Walt. [...]

_____ *LS: Say more about the role itself.*
BV: But then I think that maybe it's not about the quality of my acting.
25 It's the fact of the character being unsympathetic because of his weak-
ness. It's an odd thing, as a first time actor, to have to step into a role
that's disparaged by the script and humiliated by the other characters.
Playing him well is like making a deal with the devil. To the extent that
I did a good job, I reinforced that image of effeminate Asian guys who
30 are wimps, geeks and can't advocate for themselves.

_____ *LS: Does Thao become a man in your opinion? Does he get
stronger?*
BV: I worked on that. It wasn't easy because the scenes were shot
completely out of sequence so it was hard to get a sense of the continuity
35 and the progression. I tried to show Thao's change through the physi-
cality of my performances. I hung my head less and less. In the barber-
shop scene, I made my voice get a bit raspier and more like Eastwood's
as they tried to man me up. I threw in some sassy gestures. By the time
I was getting the job at the construction site, I added more of a swagger
40 to my walk. Things like that. [...]

_____ *LS: You've said a lot about the Asian masculinities portrayed
in mainstream media. Talk about your own background, how you were
brought up, what kind of male role models you had.*
BV: When I was young, my Dad was a very important figure in my life.
45 I was expected to follow him around to funerals and weddings and other
rituals and help him with whatever he was doing. Through him and my
other male relatives, I was learning to be strong and respectable, to
shake hands and be good with words. I saw how to be polite, especially
to elders – even to ancestors. It was very important to be able to speak
50 well, including in front of groups, and not make an ass of yourself.

11 chafe at sth.: be annoyed with sth.
11 subordination: act of making sb. less powerful
15 dignity: sense of self-worth
18 be premised on sth.: be based on sth. (an idea or theory)
19 clueless: not knowing sth.
21 abuse sb. [ə'bjuːs]: cruel verbal or physical treatment of sb.
27 disparage sth.: criticize sth. harshly in a demeaning manner
27 humiliate sb. [hjuː'mɪlieɪt]: make sb. feel stupid or ashamed
29 effeminate: (of a man) behaving like a woman (used in a disapproving way)
38 sassy (here): confident and slightly disrespectful
39 swagger: walk that shows confidence
49 ancestor: relative who lived a long time ago

_____ *LS: Would you describe these things as part of masculinity?*

BV: Yes, an alternative masculinity you could say. Y'know helping is a big part of it. There are different takes on helping. Remember the scene in Gran Torino where the old white lady neighbor spills her groceries?
55 Thao helps her pick them up, which is nice and Walt is impressed. But Thao is contrasted with two other Hmong guys who pass by her and don't help and even make humping motions behind her back. This kind of shameless macho seems more white to me and it makes Thao's helping seem more effeminate. In Walt's eyes, Thao's helping makes him a good
60 kid, but also makes him less masculine. That's the turning point, where Walt decides to make an effort to man him up. To me, it's also where Walt starts imposing his version of white masculinity on Thao. He sees that Thao has the impulse to be respectful and help. But it's not just anyone he helps. It's a senior white lady. At this point Walt also sees
65 that Thao can subordinate himself to a white person by picking up her groceries. So he decides that Thao could bend over to take Walt's instruction too.

_____ *LS: Say more about what's white about that masculinity.*

BV: In my own upbringing, helping – especially helping elders – just
70 didn't feel this way at all. It didn't have any association with femininity. My Dad is a shaman. His sons are supposed to assist him in ceremonies and it's an honor to do that. I felt that a lot growing up. We would carry his stuff and set up for him. We would bow at the right times and we would support him to make sure he was safe when he was in trance.
75 We would sacrifice chickens for him while he communicated with the spirits. I loved doing all that. I will miss it.

From: 'Gran Torino's Hmong Lead Bee Vang on Film, Race, and Masculinity: Conversations with Louisa Schein', Hmong Studies Journal, Volume 11, Spring 2010

65 subordinate oneself to sb.: put yourself into a position of being less important than sb.
71 shaman: religious leader and healer

A Hmong family

Comprehension

1 After reading, match the following subheadings with the paragraphs of the interview. Write down the letter of the subheading you chose on the lines provided in the text.

Sub-headings

A Hmong values
B Bee Vang's acting improves Thao
C Deviating from the script
D The difficulty of playing Thao convincingly

E The value of helping others
F Two views on masculinity
G What Bee Vang wants to achieve

2 **Reading** Make a list of the qualities that a man should have in Hmong culture according to the text. State also how Asian men are seen in the USA according to Bee Vang.

Analysis

3 Compare the interview with what is shown in the film. Consider the following questions:
- Apart from the scene mentioned in the interview, where are the values of Hmong masculinity shown in the film?
- Where in the film are these values contradicted by the Hmong community?

4 Read the following excerpt from the script in which Walt proposes ways to 'man Thao up' and analyse this dialogue. Why does Thao keep his replies so short?

Walt: You can get a job. You can get a job anywhere.
Thao: Like what?
Walt: Well, how about construction?
Thao: Me?
5 **Walt:** Yeah.
Thao: Construction?
Walt: Yeah.
Thao: Do you have Alzheimer's or something?
Walt: No, you can get a job in construction. I know people in the
10 trades. Of course I'd have to make a little adjustment and man you up a little bit.
Thao: Man me up?
Walt: Yeah. And I think you ought to date Miss Yum Yum, too. It'd do you a little good. You know, get the carbon off the valves.
15 *(Later, getting out of the car at the barber shop):* Now you're just gonna learn how guys talk. You just listen to the way Martin and I banter it back and forth. You okay? You are ready?
Thao: Sure.

Beyond the text

5 a Writing Work in pairs. Write a dialogue in which you continue this conversation between Thao and Walt. Instead of Thao's one-word answer at the end ('Sure.'), have him develop and share his own opinion on the topic of manhood. Have him explain to Walt what it means to be a man in Hmong culture and contrast his views with that of Walt's (→ Language help). Use information from the film and from the interview at the beginning of this section (p. 50–52).

b Speaking Perform your dialogue in class.

> **Language help**
> I feel that … · To me/to Hmong culture manhood means/is defined by … · My views on this are … · I agree/disagree … · I believe that …

C7 Realigning the stars

Making predictions

1 Watch the last few minutes of the previous segment again (01:24:58–01:29:58). How might the story go on from here?

Comprehension

2 **Listening** Read the following incomplete sentences, then watch the final segment of the film (01:29:59–end) and fill in the gaps based on what you see.

A Walt _____ his lawn.

B He takes _____.

C He goes to _____ in order to _____.

D He buys _____.

E He goes to _____.

F He cleans _____.

G He gives Thao a _____.

H He talks with Thao about _____.

I He locks _____ in the _____.

J He leaves _____ with Thao's grandmother.

K He calls up _____.

L He goes to _____'s house.

M He takes a _____ from his pocket.

N He points his _____ at _____.

O He reaches into his jacket to pull out a _____.

Analysis

3 **a** Explain Walt's plan and his reasons for acting the way he does. Do so in 3–5 sentences.
   b Compare your text with another student.
   c Find another pair of students to work with and compare your results once again.
   d Discuss any open questions in class.

4 Examine Walt's attitude towards religion in this segment, taking into account observations you made while watching the whole film.

5 Walt's actions and will, which is read at the end of the film, can be seen as a statement on his sense of belonging.
Get together in groups of four. Work with a placemat.

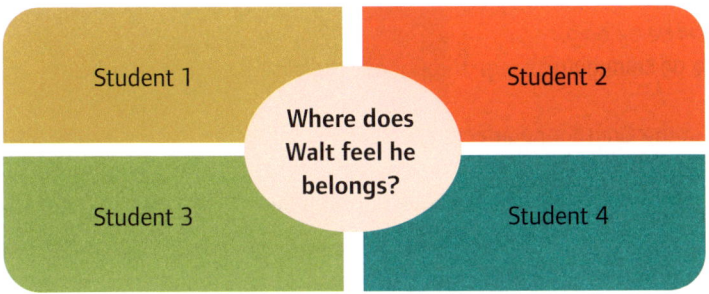

a Write down your thoughts on this question: Where does Walt feel he belongs? Compare situations when Walt's sense of belonging stayed the same to when it shifted.

b Rotate the placemat three times so that each student can read the others' thoughts and comment on them in writing.

c Together with your group, formulate a statement on Walt's sense of belonging in three sentences. These should contain the essence of all four contributions.

d Discuss how Walt 'realigned his stars'.

e Speaking Present your statements in class. Discuss any points that arise.

Beyond the text

6 Imagine that Sue and Thao are sitting together after Walt's funeral, talking about Walt and the past events. They reflect on how their lives and their sense of belonging have been affected. Work with a partner to prepare this role-play. One of you works on task **a**, the other works on task **b**. Complete tasks **c** and **d** together.

a Prepare the role of Sue (→ Language help). Consider the following questions:
  – How did she experience Walt?
  – What are her memories of the encounter with the African American gang?
  – How did she experience the Hmong gang?
  – Where does she feel she belongs?
  – How did her sense of belonging change throughout the past events?

Language help
In my experience … · My experience was … · It was a scary/difficult/happy time in my life because … · Looking back, I … · I feel like I belong/don't belong because …

b Prepare the role of Thao (→ Language help, p. 55). Consider the following questions:
- How did he experience Walt?
- How did he experience the Hmong gang?
- Where does he feel he belongs?
- How did his sense of belonging change throughout the past events?
- How has inheriting the Gran Torino affected him and his sense of belonging?

c Speaking Get together and practice the dialogue between Sue and Thao.

d Speaking Prepare to present it to the class.

C8 Working with a song

1 Listen to the theme song of the movie (01:45:42–01:51:44). What are your impressions of the song?

2 Read the lyrics of the song. It is often not necessary to understand every line of the lyrics to make sense of the text as a whole.

a Pick out lines that contain references to the film and highlight them.

b Mingle in class. Share your observations on individual lines with at least five other students. Add new lines that you agree with.

c Discuss your ideas with the class.

Gran Torino *Jamie Cullum*

So tenderly
Your story is
Nothing more
Than what you see
5 Or
What you've done
Or will become
Standing strong
Do you belong
10 In your skin
Just wondering

Gentle now
The tender breeze
Blows
15 Whispers through
My Gran Torino
Whistling another
Tired song

Engine hums
20 And bitter dreams
Grow heart locked
In a Gran Torino
It beats
A lonely rhythm
25 All night long
It beats
A lonely rhythm
All night long
It beats
30 A lonely rhythm
All night long

1 tender: gentle, careful

Realign all the stars above my head
Warning signs travel far
I drink instead on my own
35 Oh! how I've known
the battle scars and worn out beds

Gentle now a tender breeze blows
whispers through a Gran Torino
whistling another tired song

40 Engines hum and bitter dreams grow
heart locked in a Gran Torino
it beats a lonely rhythm all night long

These streets are old they shine
with the things I've known
45 and breaks through the trees
their sparkling

Your world is nothing more
than all the tiny things you've left behind

So tenderly your story is
50 nothing more than what you see
or what you've done or will become
standing strong do you belong
in your skin; just wondering

Gentle now a tender breeze blows
55 whispers through the Gran Torino
whistling another tired song
engines hum and bitter dreams grow
a heart locked in a Gran Torino
it beats a lonely rhythm all night long

60 May I be so bold and stay
I need someone to hold
that shudders my skin
their sparkling

Your world is nothing more than all the tiny
65 things you've left behind

So realign all the stars above my head
warning signs travel far
I drink instead on my own oh how I've known
the battle scars and worn out beds

70 Gentle now a tender breeze blows
whispers through the Gran Torino
whistling another tired song
engines hum and bitter dreams grow
heart locked in a Gran Torino
75 it beats a lonely rhythm all night long
it beats a lonely rhythm all night long
it beats a lonely rhythm all night long

From: 'Gran Torino', Universal Music Publishing GmbH

32 realign sth. [ˌriːəˈlaɪn]: put sth. in a new and correct position
46 sparkle (v): shine brightly
60 bold (here): not afraid, brave
62 shudder (v): shake briefly, e. g. from cold or fear

C9 Working with a film title

1 a Comment on the relevance of the film's title. Consider the
   following aspects:
   – Where in the film does the car play an important role?
   – What is the importance of the car for Walt's and Thao's sense of
     belonging?
   – Do you find the title appropriate? Give reasons.
   b Collect your ideas and discuss them with a partner.

Part D
Post-viewing activities

D1 Working with a film review

Comprehension

1 Skim the following text and tick which of the following statements is true:

> **A** The author recommends watching the film whole-heartedly, because Clint Eastwood's performance is outstanding and the plot is very convincing.
>
> **B** The author recommends watching the film, although he sees problems with the credibility of the plot.
>
> **C** The author does not recommend the film because he objects to the racism and insults expressed by the main character.
>
> **D** The author does not recommend the film because Clint Eastwood's acting is not what it used to be.
>
> line: _____ quote: _____

Thoughts on *Gran Torino* *Peter Bradshaw*

The Ford Gran Torino earned its footnote in pop culture history when a ketchup-red 75 model with a white racing stripe was featured every week in the TV cop show Starsky and Hutch. The model shown here is an earlier vintage, 1972, and its owner's glory days would appear to be from around
5 the same era. This widower, retired car worker, military veteran and seething American patriot Walt Kowalski, played with grandstanding gusto and unfakable star quality by Clint Eastwood. (Eastwood also directs and produces.) Walt bought one of the Gran Torinos that he helped to manufacture – 'right off the line' – but keeps it in pristine condition in
10 the garage, while he rumbles around town in an old Ford pickup, glowering at foreign automobiles and their disloyal American owners.

We join the story as the ageing Walt has just lost his wife and, at the funeral, has to endure the supercilious homilies of a young priest (whose religion he tolerated for his late wife's sake) along with the insolence
15 and lack of respect displayed by his smug grownup sons, both foreign-car owners, and their unspeakable teenage children. The neighborhood has gone all to hell, too. The house next door is now owned by a Hmong family – a widespread South-east Asian minority – and Walt does not trouble to distinguish them from the Koreans he fought in the 1950s, of
20 whom, we are later to learn, he despatched at least 13.

Walt is a racist; he is a resenter of the spooks, gooks and mooks, mentally lumped in with all the local criminals and gangbangers around town who are undermining decent values. The political becomes personal

4 glory days: better time in the past
5 era ['ɪərə]: particular period of time in the past
6 seething: strongly felt
6 grandstanding: (here) behaving in a way that makes people admire you
6–7 with gusto: with a lot of energy
9 pristine ['prɪstiːn]: in very good, new condition,
10–11 glower at sb.: look at sb. angrily
13 supercilious: *überheblich*
13 homily: *Moralpredigt*
14 insolence: rudeness
15 smug: self-satisfied
20 despatch sb.: (here) kill sb.
21 spook (infml): offensive word for a person of African origin
21 gook (infml): offensive word for a person of Korean origin
21 mook (infml): loser
22 gangbanger (infml): person who is a member of a gang (negative)

when Thao (Bee Vang), a shy, bookish teenage boy who lives next door
to Walt is bullied by his thuggish cousin and no-good buddies into
joining their gang. His initiation test is to bust into Walt's garage and steal
his treasured Gran Torino. Sure enough, Thao's incompetent nocturnal raid
triggers Walt's halogen security lights and Walt comes running with the
M1 assault rifle he keeps cleaned and ready – keen to bring his score up to
14. The meeting of Walt and Thao is to change both their lives.

Eastwood's performance as Walt is a treat. No one could have animated
the role like this and no one else could conceivably have got away with
the racist tirades, reactionary arias and bigoted broadsides. He gets
away with it because we know full well that he is eventually going to
reveal that great big bruised and hurting heart-of-gold hidden under
the faded grey T-shirt. [...]

Very often, Walt communicates only in a soft growl, an inchoate version
of the whispery-croaky threats and insults that are his stock in trade.
There is a bravura moment when Walt rolls past in his pickup, just as
black guys are threatening Thao's smart, feisty cousin Sue (Ahney Her),
while she is out walking with a local white boy who ingratiatingly, and
catastrophically, tries to affect gangsta style to placate them. The cranky
old grandpa faces them down and even pulls a gun, then subtly estab-
lishes his psychological mastery of the situation by making it clear he
shares the blacks' contempt for Sue's creepy pseudo-urban date: 'They're
not your "bro", and I don't blame them!'

The politics of racial insult become even more complex when Walt
takes Thao on a visit to his local barber in order to give him a masterclass
in the friendly exchange of insults traditionally performed by this 'polack'
and 'wop'. When Thao tries it, the barber is furious and from nowhere
produces a pump-action shotgun. The lesson is clear. Knockabout ethnic
comedy is OK when it is performed by your white elders and betters.

Like its hero, this movie is a great big sentimental softie under its
tough-guy persona. Still very conservative, though. The progressive re-
velation of this fact in a number of jolting plot transitions is a little tough
to take. Finally, Walt makes a confession to this baby-faced priest and
lovably admits to once kissing a lady who wasn't his wife and not paying
his taxes: no mention of threatening people with guns and pistol-whipping
a gangster, though. There is also the question of how Walt finally puts
away his nasty attitudes to minorities and becomes a better person: I'm
not sure I entirely buy this, and the transformation is questionable.

This is still an enjoyably big, brash, macho melodrama, saved from
absurdity by Eastwood's cracking performance. It isn't his late master-
piece: I think his Iwo Jima movies fit that bill better. But it is almost
certainly Clint Eastwood's final acting appearance: a must-see on that
account if nothing else.

From: 'Gran Torino', The Guardian, 20 February 2009

25 thuggish: violent, aggressive
27 nocturnal: happening at night
29 score: (here) number of Asian people Walt has killed
32 conceivable [kənˈsiːvəbl]: believable
33 tirade: long, angry speech
33 bigoted [ˈbɪɡətɪd]: strongly prejudiced
33 broadside: strong criticism
37 inchoate [ɪnˈkəʊət] (adj): just beginning to develop
40 feisty [ˈfaɪsti]: strong, determined
40 The author mistakenly refers to Sue as Thao's cousin. She is his sister.
41 ingratiating [ɪnˈɡreɪʃieɪtɪŋ]: intended to make others accept you
42 placate sb.: make sb. stop feeling angry
45 contempt: feeling of having no respect for sb.
49 polack (infml): offensive word for a person of Polish origin
50 wop (infml): offensive word for a person of Italian origin
51 knockabout (adj): deliberately silly
55 jolt (v): make a sudden movement
62 brash: in a way that shows too much confidence
64 Iwo Jima: Japanese island, battle site in World War II

Clint Eastwood, director and actor in Gran Torino, *at the LA Athletics Club in Los Angeles in 2014.*

2 Say whether the following statements are true or false. Support your answer by giving a quotation from the text (with line numbers).

Statement	True	False
A To Walt Kowalski, members of different Asian communities are pretty much the same.	○	○
line: _____ quote: _____		
B Walt has a particularly negative attitude towards the Asian youths who are causing trouble in the neighborhood.	○	○
line: _____ quote: _____		
C Only Clint Eastwood can afford to play a racist such as Walt Kowalski.	○	○
line: _____ quote: _____		
D It is clear to the viewers that, at the end, Kowalski is going to show better human qualities than he did at the beginning of the film.	○	○
line: _____ quote: _____		
E Clint Eastwood is famous for the way he speaks.	○	○
line: _____ quote: _____		
F Walt shows that he is in control of the situation in many ways, such as scaring the African American youths.	○	○
line: _____ quote: _____		
G At the barbershop Thao learns that you should make racial jokes when talking with older white men.	○	○
line: _____ quote: _____		
H The author rates older films made by Clint Eastwood higher than *Gran Torino*.	○	○
line: _____ quote: _____		

Analysis

3 The table below contains elements that all film reviews should have. Identify examples of these elements in the text and give line references.

Elements of a film review	Line number(s)
a catchy introduction	
a description of the central topic of the film	
information on the characters	
information on the setting	
a plot summary (incomplete, the ending should not be revealed)	
general and (possibly) background information on the director, producer and actors/actresses	
opinion on the film/recommendation	

D2 Writing a film review

1 Write your own review of the film *Gran Torino* with the title: 'Gran Torino – The Ambiguity of Belonging'.
  a Collect ideas. Consider different characters (Walt, Thao, Sue, Spider, etc.) and some areas in which they belong or struggle to belong (e.g. family, neighborhood, religion, gangs, names, gender, work, material values, symbols of belonging, etc.). Do not try to cover all characters or areas. Instead, select those that are most important to you.
  b Sort your ideas into paragraphs that contain the relevant elements of a review.
  c Writing Write your review.
  d In a group of four, exchange your reviews and give each other feedback (your teacher will provide you with suitable feedback forms).

Module III

Crooked Letter, Crooked Letter

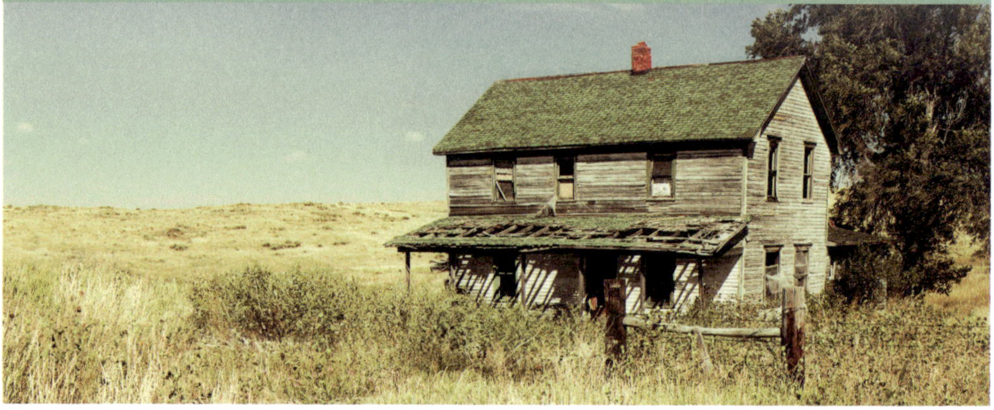

Part A
Pre-reading activities

A1 Pictures

The pictures below illustrate aspects of the novel you are going to read.

A

B

C

D

E

F

G

H

I

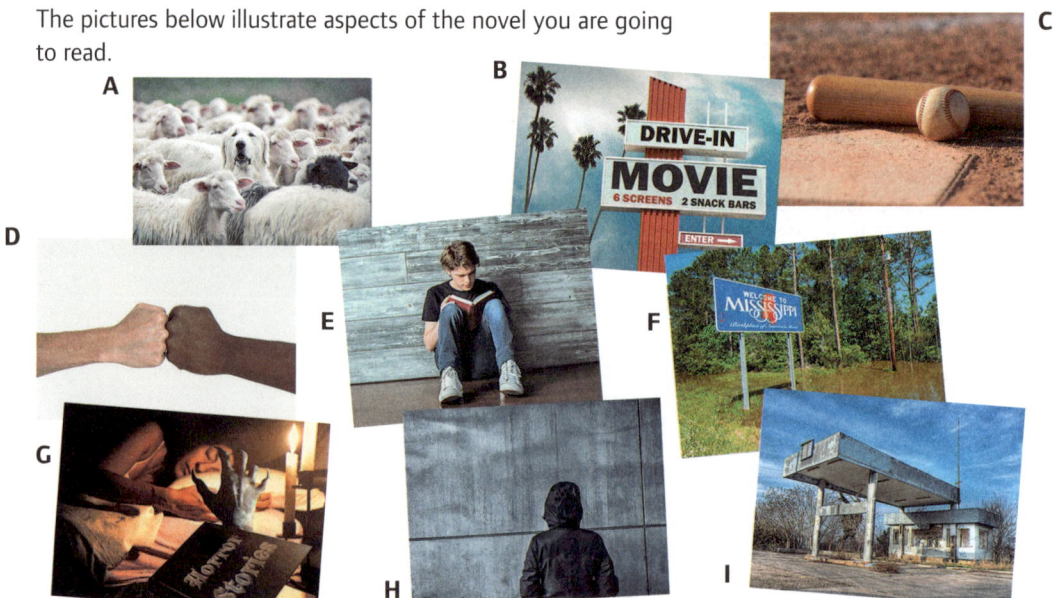

1 **Think:** Choose one of the pictures and do some brainstorming.
   Note down everything that comes to your mind.
2 **Pair:** Work with a partner who has chosen the same picture and
   discuss the words or expressions you have found.
   Agree on the five most relevant items.
3 **Share:** Work with another pair and look at their pictures.
   Present your ideas to each other.

A2 Working with words

The concepts of *ambiguity* and *belonging* play an important role
in *Crooked Letter, Crooked Letter*. Work with a partner. One of you
works on task **1**, the other on task **2**. Then both go on to task **3**.
1 Look up the word *ambiguity* and its word family in a monolingual
   dictionary.
   a Make a sentence with each of the words you found.
   b Think of a situation, a phrase, a statement that seemed
      ambiguous to you.
2 Look up the word *belong* and its word family in a monolingual
   dictionary.
   a Make a sentence with each of the words you found.
   b What does belonging mean to you? Name situations in which you
      felt you belonged to a place or a person.
3 Tell your partner what you found out.

A3 A mental video

Close your eyes. Your teacher will read out a short passage from
the novel to you.
1 Try to visualize the scene in front of your eyes.
2 Tell a partner what you saw, heard and felt.

A4 Understanding the background

1 Form six groups. Each group does some research on one of
   the following topics and prepares a short presentation on it:

A the American Civil Rights Movement

B Jim Crow laws

D segregation in the US

C busing/redistricting in the US

E Mississippi

F the American South

2 Speaking Get together in new groups so that there is a representative for each topic in each of the groups. Give your presentation to your group members and take notes on theirs.

A5 Personalizing

1 Look at the following word bank and make sure you understand all the words.

> struggle to belong · a sense of belonging · be a role model · bond with sb. · crave sth. · strive for sth. · call sb. names · shun sb. · cause high/low self-esteem · find ways to belong · feel left out/excluded · create a feeling of belonging · experience · connect with others · feel highly valued · discriminate against sb. · feel discouraged · empathetic · establish one's self-esteem · exclude sb. from sth. · avoid sb. · social acceptance/rejection · experience social exclusion/prejudice · feel alienated from sb./sth. · face painful experiences/emotions · be understanding · feel included · cope with sth. · share interests · reject sb. · confident/self-conscious about sth. · feel a (strong) need/desire to … · label sb. sth. · feel embarrassed · bully sb. · suffer from / experience discrimination/alienation · be disconnected from sb./sth. · feel ostracized · supportive · threaten sb.'s identity · trustworthy · feel unworthy · have strong social bonds · helpful · feel connected to sb./sth. · peer group · feel encouraged/discouraged · receive attention/support · relate to sb. · feel ridiculed · reliable · seek acceptance with sb./approval from sb. · sensitive · stigmatize sb. · have strong/weak relationships · feel attached to a place/person/group

  a Make a mindmap containing all the words. You may structure your mindmap by language or by topic.
  b Add more words if you like.
  c Compare your mindmap with a partner.
2 Use your mindmap from task **1** to discuss the following questions with a partner or in a group:
  a Have you ever felt humiliated by others? How? Why? How did you react?
  b What makes people humiliate others?
  c What makes a friend a friend? Name five character traits a good friend should have. Be able to explain why you think so.
  d What makes people become outsiders?

A6 Quotes

1 Read the following quotes taken from the novel.
Say what they tell you about
  a the characters
  b the setting
  c the theme(s)
  d the main conflict(s).

A

'The Rutherford girl had been missing
for eight days when Larry Ott returned
home and found a monster waiting
in his house.'

B

'He understood that Carl liked most
(= almost) everyone except him.'

C

'He wondered how broken Larry was by the events
of his life, how damaged. What would Silas tell
him if he ever woke up? Sometimes he couldn't help
but wish he wouldn't.'

D

'But that was his trouble, wasn't it?
Letting himself off the hook had been
his way of life.'

E

'Silas felt flattened by the truth, or the
telling of it, his lungs empty and raw and
the spaces behind his eyes throbbing.'

F

'The land had a way of covering
the wrongs of people.'

A7 Wrapping things up

1 Write a short text describing what you can guess about the
novel you are going to read. Consider the results of the tasks you
have worked on so far.
Make sure to cover the following aspects:
  − the characters
  − the setting
  − the theme(s)
  − the main conflict(s).

Part B
While-reading activities

B1 Working with a reading log

When reading a novel with a challenging structure it is useful to keep a reading log. It will help you to reconstruct the chronology of events while reading.

Use the columns in the middle and on the right to take notes on everything that strikes you, e. g. the characters, the setting, the language, topics or quotes.

Always indicate page(s) and line(s) so you will be able to find things easily later on.

Chapter(s) and topics	What happens when and where?	Things worth thinking about (e. g. topics, characters, …)	Words worth remembering (page/line)
Chapters 1–2: Getting to know Larry and Silas			
Chapter 3: Larry and Silas's childhood			
Chapters 4–5: …			
Chapter 6: …			
…			

B2 Getting to know Larry and Silas
(chapters 1–2)

Comprehension

1 Read chapter 1 and choose whether the following statements are
true or false. Indicate page and line(s) in the text and give a quote.

Statement	True	False
A One morning Larry drives back home because he forgot something he needs at the shop.	○	○
page/line: _____ quote: _____		
B He is 41 years old, single and lives in his parents' house.	○	○
page/line: _____ quote: _____		
C He took great care in building a moveable pen for his chickens.	○	○
page/line: _____ quote: _____		
D Larry runs a garage which is mainly frequented by the locals.	○	○
page/line: _____ quote: _____		
E The previous day, Chief Investigator French came to see Larry at his house because he usually drives too fast.	○	○
page/line: _____ quote: _____		

2 Read chapter 2 and choose whether the following statements are true or false. Indicate page and line(s) in the text and give a quote.

Statement	True	False
A Constable Silas Jones sets out to look for Morton Morrisette, with whom he used to play basketball in high school.	○	○
page/line: _____ quote: _____		
B Later in the afternoon he wants to go and pay Larry a visit.	○	○
page/line: _____ quote: _____		
C He remembers a message Larry left on his answering machine a week ago.	○	○
page/line: _____ quote: _____		
D There is nobody at the shop and Silas wonders where Larry might be.	○	○
page/line: _____ quote: _____		
E While thinking about the past Silas gets a call and is told to go assist a person who has been bitten by a rattlesnake.	○	○
page/line: _____ quote: _____		
F Silas's girlfriend Angie calls and says that she has been sent to Larry's house.	○	○
page/line: _____ quote: _____		

3 Work with a partner. One of you works on task **a**, the other one on task **b**. Then go on to task **c** and compare results.
  a Collect factual information about Larry.
  b Collect factual information about Silas.
  c Exchange your results and compare your findings with another pair.

4 What is your impression of Larry and Silas?

Analysis

5 a Work with a partner to make sure you know the meaning of the words in the box below.

> ambitious · caring · cheerful · childish · compassionate · dutiful · evasive · fragile · grown-up · helpful · hypocritical · ingenious · isolated · knowledgeable · likeable · modest · moody · narrow-minded · offensive · open · outgoing · perseverant · phoney · polite · querulous · ruthless · self-confident · self-conscious · sensible · sensitive · shy · smart · stoic · straightforward · timid · understanding · vicious

  b Describe Silas and Larry's characters. Use adjectives from the box. Justify your choice with the help of your findings from task **3**.

6 Speaking Which of the two would you rather like to have as
 a a friend or
 b an opponent?
 Give a two-minute speech to a partner.
7 Look at the following photos.
 a Choose the one that illustrates chapters 1 and 2 best.
 b Speaking Discuss your choice with a partner and agree
 on one photo.

A

B

C

D

Making predictions: chapter 3
8 Speculate: Which of the following statements might be true?
 Say why you think so.

> **Chapter 3 will provide some more information about …**
> **A** who shot Larry.
> **B** Larry and Silas's friendship when they were boys.
> **C** the relationship between Mr and Mrs Ott.
> **D** why Silas never answered Larry's first phone call.

B3 Larry and Silas's childhood (chapter 3)

Comprehension

1 Read chapter 3.
   a Divide the chapter into passages to go with the headings A–G in the table below. Be careful: they are not in the correct order.
   b Number the headings in the correct order and write page and line references in the right column.

Heading	Number	Page/Line
A Saturday at the garage	_____	_____
B Joining the club	_____	_____
C Out in the freezing cold	_____	_____
D Finding Silas	_____	_____
E You don't take after me	_____	_____
F Two old coats	_____	_____
G One Sunday afternoon	_____	_____

Analysis

2 Describe how Larry feels about being bused to another, predominantly Black school.
3 Examine Larry's social ties, e. g. with family or friends. Also refer back to chapters 1 and 2.
4 Work in groups of four. Your teacher will assign a character from the book to each of you.
   a Choose different situations from chapter 3 and describe how your character might have felt in this situation. Be able to explain why you think so. → Language help
   b Present your results to the other group members.

Language help
accepted · annoyed · broken · cheerful · curious · desperate · elated · furious · humiliated · inferior · inquisitive · joyous · lighthearted · lonely · miserable · optimistic · outraged · proud · rejected · stunned · superior · surprised · troubled · uneasy · vulnerable

B4 Why busing didn't end school segregation

Audie Cornish

In the 1970s and 1980s, many children in the USA went to schools where they were part of the ethnic minority, just like Larry. One reason for this was the concept of 'busing' (→ Info box).

> **Info Busing**
> In the United States, busing means transporting students to schools further away from their homes in order to prevent residential segregation: by busing them to schools, authorities intended students from different ethnic groups to mix.
> In 1954 racial segregation in public schools was already declared unconstitutional in the USA. But only in the 1970s and 1980s did many school districts implement compulsory busing plans. A few of these plans are still in use today. Yet in the late 1980s, busing declined. One of the reasons was that the schools were too far away from students' homes and students spent too much time on the bus even though suitable schools were available in their neighborhoods. Many parents who could afford it sent their children to private or parochial schools to avoid busing schemes.
> By the early 1990s, most school districts had stopped using compulsory busing to desegregate schools. However, many continued to provide a school bus service because families had become accustomed to the transportation programs.

1 Think of the region you live in or of other regions in Germany: Could a concept like busing be useful? What might be its benefits? Who might be in favor of it? Who might be against it?

2 **Listening** 🌐 SPT354924-1 Listen to part 1 of the audio text and tick the correct answer(s). Sometimes more than one answer is possible.

Annotations
legacy (adj): still in use
envision sth.: *etwas für möglich halten*
backlash (n): strong negative reaction by a large number of people
zoning: process of dividing parts of a city into zones used for different purposes
wherewithal: *die nötigen Mittel*

a What is METCO?

    A a voluntary program that intended to promote desegregation
    B a program that bused Black children to white Boston suburbs
    C a family program that was invented by the Metropolitan Council
    D a voluntary school program for white parents

line: _____ quote: _____

b The program …

   A is funded by the local school authorities.
   B pays the towns about 5,000 $ per child.
   C soon celebrates its 50th anniversary.
   D will be stopped in a couple of years.

line: _____ quote: _____

c Initially the program was about …

   A giving white children access to schools in the suburbs.
   B giving Black children access to better schools.
   C letting white parents participate in the integration movement.
   D no longer letting white parents hinder the integration movement.

line: _____ quote: _____

d METCO students …

   A have a 90 percent college graduation rate.
   B achieve higher scores on state tests than students in public schools.
   C achieve almost the same results as in the past.
   D have conflicting views about their results as adults.

line: _____ quote: _____

e Former METCO students say the following about their schools:

   A They suffered from discrimination there.
   B They felt it was nice to be there.
   C They felt like guests at someone else's house there.
   D They were never allowed to use the refrigerator there.

line: _____ quote: _____

f A student says that due to taking part in the METCO program …

   A she may be a little over-confident.
   B she does not see any limits in her life.
   C she still finds it difficult to say what she thinks.
   D she does not mind being the only Black person in most environments now.

line: _____ quote: _____

3 `Listening` 🌐 SPT354924-2 Listen to part 2 of the audio text, then say whether the following statements are true or false.

Annotations
charter school: (in the US) school which receives money from the state, but which operates separately from the state system
magnet school: (in the US) school that offers extra courses to attract students from other areas of the city
sustain sth.: keep sth. up
white flight: large-scale migration of white people from racially mixed urban regions
hand down a decision: *die Entscheidung einem untergeordneten Gericht übermitteln*
when push comes to shove: *wenn es hart auf hart kommt*

Statement	True	False
A Some parents prefer charter schools as alternatives to busing programs.	○	○
B Charter schools are quite successful at fighting racial isolation.	○	○
C Busing programs often failed because there weren't enough white children to take part in it.	○	○
D Black students suffered a lot from the disadvantages of busing.	○	○
E Communities tried to introduce measures like redrawing zoning lines to desegregate schools.	○	○
F Most parents who consider themselves liberal are willing to send their children to schools with many Black students.	○	○

4 Explain what effect busing has or had on Black students as far as their feeling of belonging is concerned.

Making predictions: chapter 4

5 Make some guesses and tick the best answer. Say why you think so.

  a When Silas and CI French inspect Larry's house they …

   ○ **A** find important clues as to who might have shot Larry.
   ○ **B** find nothing at all.
   ○ **C** find tracks of a tall man's shoes that disappear in the woods.

  b In a flashback Larry remembers a situation in which he …

   ○ **A** called Silas a n****r and this ended their friendship.
   ○ **B** was beaten up by his father.
   ○ **C** spied on Cindy with Silas.

B5 Father and son (chapters 4–5)

Comprehension

1 Read chapters 4 and 5, then say who 'someone' in the following
  sentences is:

A Someone is relieved.

B Someone remembers a scene from a long time ago.

C Someone thinks that someone else is a strange person.

D Someone left a message.

E Someone is in a good mood.

F Someone was confused.

G Someone is worried about losing someone.

H Someone shares a secret with someone else.

I Someone is courageous.

J Someone is angry.

K Someone is very mean.

L Someone feels humiliated.

Analysis

2 Revise chapters 1–3 with the help of your reading log, then work in groups of three. Each of you works on task **a**, **b** or **c** and makes notes. Then go on to task **3**.
On the basis of chapters 1–5 examine …

  a Larry and Silas's role and position in society.

  b Larry and Silas's friendship.

  c the relationship between Larry and his father.

3 In your group, exchange results.

Beyond the text

4 Choose one of the situations from chapters 3 and 5 in which Larry is an outsider. Imagine you are Larry, looking back at these times.

  a Writing Write Larry's interior monologue (→ Info box, p. 19) in which he imagines what he could have done differently to belong.

  b Speaking Read out your monologue and listen to other students reading theirs. Which monologue is most convincing? Say why.

5 a Writing Write a letter to Silas or to Mr Ott telling them what you think of their behavior and asking them questions about it.

  b Writing Your teacher will give you one of your classmates' letters. Put yourself in the position of Silas or Mr Ott and answer it.

Making predictions: chapter 6

6 In chapter 6 the reader will learn a lot about Silas. In the following sentences, choose the word(s) that you think is/are correct and write it/them on the lines:

A Silas finds **a joint/a porn magazine/dirty clothes** at Larry's house.

_____

B Silas finds out that his mother knew **Larry/Mr Ott when he was a baby/a young man**.

_____

C Silas grew up in **Mississippi/Chicago/Alabama**.

_____

D When Silas was a boy, he and his mother led a **pleasant/poverty-stricken/dangerous life**.

_____

E Silas **steals/finds/hides** an important piece of evidence at Larry's house.

_____

B6 North and South (chapter 6)

Comprehension

1 The following chunks summarize the flashback in chapter 6.
Put them in the correct order by writing numbers in the bubbles.

A Alice and Silas take the bus and go south to Mississippi. On their first stop in Memphis, Alice has to sell part of her belongings at a pawn shop because she cannot carry everything she has taken with her.

B Someone steals Silas's backpack, his pocket knife, his coat and even his shoes. When Silas, his mother and the driver return to the truck, they notice that all their belongings have been stolen.

C In Jackson, Mississippi, Larry understands that his mother does not really know where to go. The bus driver offers them a ride in his pick-up truck, which Alice finally accepts.

D In the morning Alice and Silas arrive in Fulsom, Mississippi, where they get off the truck and go to a diner. Alice is angry and refuses to talk to Silas. She tells him that she intends to go to a town near Chabot where she knows someone.

E One day Alice's boyfriend is arrested. Alice bails him out of prison, but he tells her to sell all her belongings and leave because he has committed another crime and he knows that the police are after him.

F Silas is furious and wants to go back home to Chicago. Once the car stops at a traffic light, Silas jumps off and runs away to hide behind garbage cans.

G Alice asks Silas to leave her alone for a while. In Chabot an old man picks them up and takes them to a store. From there they walk along a dirt road until they reach a hunting cabin in the woods. Alice tells her son to collect wood.

H When Silas was thirteen years old he lived with his mother and her boyfriend Oliver in an all-Black neighborhood in Chicago's South Side.

2 Begin a list of things, hints or events in the novel that might help Silas find the man who shot Larry. Continue the list while reading the novel. Make some guesses: who tried to kill Larry?

Analysis

3 Explain the following quote in the context of the chapter:

> 'It was a world he wanted no part of. He wanted no part of her.' (p. 125, l. 3)

4 Explain why Silas decides to jump off the pick-up truck.

B7 Die Große Migration *Nikolaus Piper*

1 Mediation Work on task **a** or **b**, which will be assigned to you
by your teacher.
  a Summarize the push factors that made African Americans leave
the South and be prepared to inform your partner about them.
  b Summarize the pull factors that made African Americans leave the
South and be prepared to inform your partner about them.

> **Info Push and pull factors**
> There are many reasons that make people leave their country/region and migrate
> to another.
> Factors existing in their region/country of origin, i.e. factors that force people out,
> are called **push factors**: poverty, fear, unemployment, persecution, war, climate change.
> Factors existing in the region/country they are moving to, i.e. factors that attract
> people, are called **pull factors**: safety, employment, opportunity, (religious) freedom,
> political stability.

**Vor 100 Jahren begann die Wanderung der Schwarzen aus
den amerikanischen Südstaaten in die Industriestädte des Nordens.
Die Parallelen zum heutigen Europa sind offenkundig.**

„Sie verließen ihre Heimat, als wollten sie einem Fluch entfliehen. Sie
waren bereit, fast alles zu opfern, um ein Bahnticket zu bekommen. Und
sie gingen mit der Absicht zu bleiben." Es sind nicht syrische Flüchtlinge
auf dem Bahnhof von Budapest, von denen hier die Rede ist. Der
5 Publizist Emmet J. Scott beschreibt so die Stimmung auf Bahnhöfen in
den Südstaaten der USA während der „Großen Migration". Gut sechs
Millionen Schwarze flohen damals vor Not, Rassentrennung und
Lynchjustiz im Süden nach New York, Chicago, Detroit und in andere
Industriestädte des Nordens. Die große Flüchtlingsbewegung begann
10 um das Jahr 1915 und endete 1970 nach dem Sieg der amerikanischen
Bürgerrechtsbewegung.
    Die Große Migration, noch immer oft unterschätzt, veränderte das
Gesicht der USA. Vor 1915 lebten 90 Prozent aller Afroamerikaner im
Süden, 1970 waren es noch die Hälfte. Und wenn ein historisches

15 Ereignis Parallelen zur heutigen Flüchtlingskrise in Europa hat, dann ist
es die Große Migration. Sie war anders, weil sie in einer Nation stattfand;
es gab keine Sprachprobleme und keine Grenzen, die man hätte schlie-
ßen können. Aber sie birgt auch Lehren für die Gegenwart – darüber,
wie komplex Integration ist und dass deren Erfolg letztlich von der
20 Ökonomie abhängt.

Ein Blick zurück: Nach ihrem Sieg im Bürgerkrieg 1865 wollten die
Nordstaaten den Süden zunächst vollkommen neu aufbauen. Bestimmen
sollten dort nur befreite Sklaven und Weiße, die sich eindeutig gegen
die Sklaverei stellten. Gegen dieses Programm der „Reconstruction"
25 wehrten sich die alten Eliten mit Obstruktion und mit dem Terror des
Ku-Klux-Klan. Letztlich hatten sie Erfolg. In den 1880er- und 1890er-
Jahren erließen alle Südstaaten Rassegesetze, die Schwarze zu Bürgern
zweiter Klasse machten. Sie wurden ihres Wahlrechts beraubt, sie durften
nicht neben Weißen sitzen, ihre Kinder gingen auf schlechte Schulen.
30 Die Stadt Mobile (Alabama) untersagte es 1909 Schwarzen, nach 22 Uhr
noch ihre Wohnungen zu verlassen. [...]

Fest steht, dass der Erste Weltkrieg den Zug nach Norden richtig in
Gang setzte. Mit Ausbruch der Feindseligkeiten in Europa riss der Strom
der Einwanderer aus Polen, Irland, Deutschland und Italien plötzlich ab.
35 Die rapide wachsende Industrie im Norden litt unter akutem Arbeits-
kräftemangel. Die Autohersteller in Detroit gingen dabei 1915 einen
ungewöhnlichen Schritt: „Sie schickten Werber bis nach South Carolina,
um dort weiße und schwarze Arbeiter anzuheuern", sagt Joel Stone,
Kurator bei der Historischen Gesellschaft Detroit. „So etwas hatte es
40 zuvor noch nie gegeben." Mit dieser Aktion waren Detroit, Chicago,

Workers working on an assembly line of cars in Detroit

New York, Cleveland und all die anderen Industriestädte im Norden für die unterdrückten Schwarzen kein Traum mehr, sondern eine konkrete Chance. Anders als heute entwickelten sich Migration und Arbeitsangebot parallel.

45 Die Autoindustrie im frühen 20. Jahrhundert war überdies ideal für die Aufnahme von Migranten. An den Fließbändern gab es relativ gut bezahlte Jobs, die aber keine sehr hohe Qualifikation verlangten. Im Durchschnitt konnte ein Schwarzer in einer Fabrik des Nordens dreimal so viel verdienen wie als Landarbeiter im Süden. In der berühmten
50 River-Rouge-Fabrik von Ford in Detroit arbeiteten zeitweise mehr als 90 000 Männer. General Motors, Ford, Chrysler und American Motors machten die Migration möglich, sie wurden auch dank der Migranten groß. […]

Weiße wehrten sich dagegen, dass schwarze Familien in ihre
55 Wohnviertel zogen. […] Anders als bei anderen Einwandern lag bei ihnen kein Ozean zwischen ihrer Heimat und Amerika. „Es gab keine Möglichkeit, die Flut der Schwarzen aus dem Süden zu stoppen." Das machte Angst.

Am Ende zogen sich die Schwarzen in eigene Ghettos zurück: die
60 Southside von Chicago, Harlem in New York, Highland Park in Detroit. Diese neue Rassentrennung schuf soziale Probleme, die zum Teil bis heute nicht gelöst sind.

Trotz aller Ressentiments – die Große Migration veränderte die USA von Grund auf. Zum ersten Mal griffen die Nachfahren der afrikanischen
65 Sklaven aktiv in die Geschichte des Landes ein. Das schuf ein neues Selbstbewusstsein. In New York entstand die Harlem Renaissance, eine Erneuerungsbewegung schwarzer Künstler und Schriftsteller während der 1920er-Jahre. Schließlich brachten die Schwarzen nicht nur ihre Arbeitskraft mit, sondern auch ihre Musik. Blues und Jazz waren zwar
70 schon vor 1915 aus New Orleans nach Chicago gekommen, doch erst die Große Migration schuf die Voraussetzungen dafür, dass beide zu einem globalen Phänomen werden konnten: Musikclubs und ein ebenso verständiges wie zahlungskräftiges Publikum. Auch junge Weiße begannen sich für Jazz zu interessieren.

75 Louis Armstrong (1901–1971), der größte Jazzmusiker der Geschichte, wurde in ärmlichen Verhältnissen in New Orleans geboren. Seine Großeltern waren Sklaven gewesen. Armstrong spielte dort als Gelegenheitsmusiker Flügelhorn und Trompete. Schließlich setzte er sich 1922, wie viele andere, in den Zug nach Chicago. Er folgte dem Ruf
80 seines Mentors Joe „King" Oliver schloss sich dessen Creole Jazz Band an. In Chicago konnte Armstrong es sich leisten, ausschließlich von der Musik zu leben und begann so seine Weltkarriere. Viele andere Stars aus der Frühzeit des Jazz haben die Große Migration nach Chicago mitgemacht: Sidney Bechet, Jelly Roll Morton, Lee Collins, Wilbur Sweatman.

85 **Der Verlust von sechs Millionen Menschen war ein Schock für den Süden.**

Die Migration hatte auch tragische Folgen. Ein Beispiel ist Detroit. Die Stadt zeigt, dass sich Fehler bei der Wohnungspolitik für Migranten bitter rächen können. Nach den Jahren des Booms – die Zahl der
90 Einwohner stieg von 465 000 Einwohnern 1910 bis auf 1,9 Millionen 1950 – begann ein beispielloser Niedergang. Weiße und wohlhabende Schwarze zogen in die Vorstädte, die mit dem Auto jetzt leicht zu erreichen waren. In Detroit zurück blieben arme Schwarze. Sie zahlten wenige oder keine Steuern, wodurch die Stadt immer mehr verkam. Nach
95 schweren Rassenunruhen 1967 flohen die letzten Weißen. Dann kam in den Siebzigerjahren noch die Krise der amerikanischen Autoindustrie dazu, die mit der Konkurrenz aus Deutschland und Japan nicht umgehen konnte. Heute hat Detroit noch 770 000 Einwohner, ist bettelarm, die Schulen sind miserabel, und der frühere Bürgermeister Kwame
100 Kilpatrick sitzt wegen Korruption im Gefängnis. […]

Und noch eine Folge der Großen Migration: Der Verlust von sechs Millionen Menschen war ein Schock für die Wirtschaft des Südens. Umgekehrt wurde der Norden gezwungen, sich mit den Zuständen im Süden zu befassen. So legte die Migration die Grundlage für die Bür-
105 gerrechtsbewegung der 1950er- und 1960er-Jahre. Isabel Wilkerson schreibt: Die Große Migration „zwang den Süden, in sich zu gehen und letztlich sein feudales Kastensystem aufzugeben". Ob allerdings die heutigen Flüchtlingsströme irgendwann auch so positiv auf die Herkunftsländer rückwirken werden, ist nicht abzusehen.

From: Süddeutsche Zeitung, *24 December 2015*

2 Work with someone who worked on the other subtask to task **1** and exchange your findings.

3 Relate the information from the text to Silas's life.

4 Explain in what way this migration is different to present forms of migration to Europe.

Making predictions: chapter 7

5 Fill the gaps with a word or part of a sentence:

A _____ asks Larry out on a date.

B When picking up his date, Larry is brutally hurt by _____.

C Larry is utterly disappointed when the girl tells him that _____

_____.

D The date changes Larry's life: After it, he _____.

B8 The date (chapters 7–8)

Comprehension

1 Read chapter 7.

   a Relate the following adjectives to a character and a situation. Some
   adjectives might apply to more than one character or situation.

Adjective	Character	Situation (p./l.)
excited		
brutal		
disappointed		
worried		
isolated		

   b Find two more adjectives. Ask your partner to relate them
   to a character and/or a situation from the chapter.

2 Read chapter 8 and complete the sentence endings.
They are in chronological order.

   A Silas meets Angie and they _____.

   B Silas also talks about _____.

   C As a boy, he missed Chicago but then he _____

   _____.

   D He tells Angie that Larry has always been _____

   _____.

   E Silas remembers a situation when Larry _____

   _____.

   F Angie asks Silas if he ever _____.

   G Later Silas goes to see Larry in hospital. Larry is still _____

   _____.

H Afterwards Silas goes to the retirement home to _____

_____.

I The nurse there tells him that _____.

J He tries to make Mrs Ott understand who he is, but _____

_____.

K Silas realizes one thing about his father, namely that _____

_____.

L Silas gets back into the car. On his way to Larry's house, he _____

_____.

M Silas parks his car at Larry's house and _____.

Analysis

3 Re-read p. 152, l. 8 to p. 154, l. 10. Together with a partner, work on
tasks **a** and **b**. Then one of you chooses task **c**, the other one works
on task **d**. Then do task **e** together.
 a Briefly summarize this passage.
 b Analyse its narrative perspective (→ Info box).

> **Info Narrative perspective and point of view**
> The point of view of a narrative is the perspective from which the story is told.
> The point of view of a first-person narrator is easy to identify: the narrator tells the story
> from his or her own perspective. However, a third-person narrator can also tell a story
> from a character's point of view by focusing on what that character can see, hear and
> maybe even think. The concepts of narrator and point of view are closely related:
>
> A **first-person narrator** can only have
> – a **limited point of view**: a character in the story can't possibly know everything that's
>   going on. The reader's view is limited by what the character sees and wants to tell.
>
> A **third-person narrator** can have
> – a **limited point of view**: the narrator may be limited to the experience of one or
>   more characters in the story, or maybe he or she doesn't know the characters'
>   thoughts and feelings.
> – an **unlimited point of view**: This omniscient narrator doesn't follow any one character,
>   but moves around, entering into different characters' minds whenever he or she wants.

At a drive-in cinema

c   Imagine you are Larry waiting for Cindy to return. Re-write this passage from a first-person point of view.

d   Imagine you are a fly trapped in Larry's car. You are not able to read human thoughts or facial expressions. You watch Larry while he is driving around, stopping, waiting. Describe precisely what you observe.

e   Read your texts out to each other and compare them to the original. Explain the effect the different narrative perspectives have on you, the reader. → Language help

Language help
– This (part of the) story/novel / this excerpt is narrated in the third/first person/ told from X's perspective / the point of view of ...
– The narrator is omniscient/reliable/unreliable
– The narrator is (not) a character in the story ...
– The narrator has a limited/unlimited point of view ...
– The narrator views events from a distance.
– The narrator wants to manipulate/influence the reader by ... / because ...
– The narrator guides the reader by ...
– The reader identifies with / can easily identify with / dislikes ... / shares the protagonist's dislike for / fear of ...

4   Explain the relevance the date has to Larry's life.

Beyond the text

5   Writing Write a letter to Larry to help and support him after Cindy's disappearance. Tell him what his strengths are and why he should not give up or despair.

6 a Look up the words *loneliness* and *solitude* in a monolingual
dictionary.
   b Explain the difference in meaning in your own words.
   c Read the following quotes, then choose the one you like best.
Say why.

A

> 'I never found the companion that was so companionable
> as solitude. We are for the most part more lonely
> when we go abroad among men than when we stay
> in our chambers.'
>   Henry David Thoreau

B

> 'Solitude shows us
> what should be;
> society shows us what
> we are.'   Robert Cecil

C

> 'The great omission in American life is solitude; not loneliness, for
> this is an alienation that thrives most in the midst of crowds, but
> that zone of time and space, free from the outside pressures,
> which is the incubator of the spirit.'   Marya Mannes

D

> 'What a commentary on civilization, when being alone is being
> suspect; when one has to apologize for it, make excuses, hide the fact
> that one practices it – like a secret vice.'   Anne Morrow Lindbergh

   d Rephrase the quote in your own words.
   e Relate your quote to a character and/or a situation in chapter 7
or 8. Be able to explain your choice.
   f Get together with someone who chose another quote and
exchange your results.

Making predictions: chapter 9

7 When Larry is 41 years old he becomes acquainted with a man called
Wallace Stringfellow. Which of the following options are true?

   A Wallace is the friend Larry has always been looking for.
   B Wallace is a dubious character whose intentions are unclear.
   C Wallace will help Larry find his place back in the local community.
   D Wallace knows something about Cindy's case that has a tremendous influence
   on Larry's life.

B9 Larry and Wallace – two unlikely friends
(chapter 9)

Comprehension

1 Read chapter 9, then tick the correct answers in the boxes below and give page/line references. Only one answer is correct.

  a When Larry is in his early thirties he notices that …

      ○ **A** a boy is reading a novel in his barn.
      ○ **B** someone has been stealing items from his barn.
      ○ **C** a boy goes fishing in his pond.
      ○ **D** someone has secretly used his monster mask.

    page/line: _____ quote: _____

  b When Larry is in his early forties he …

      ○ **A** hires Wallace Stringfellow to install a TV satellite dish.
      ○ **B** gets to know Wallace Stringfellow, who wants to sell him a gun.
      ○ **C** gets to know Wallace Stringfellow, who pretends not to know anything about Larry's past.
      ○ **D** tells Wallace Stringfellow that he lied to him the first time they met.

    page/line: _____ quote: _____

  c Wallace …

      ○ **A** drinks quite a lot.
      ○ **B** breeds dogs.
      ○ **C** sells drugs to M&M.
      ○ **D** convinces Larry to buy a gun.

    page/line: _____ quote: _____

  d One day Wallace …

      ○ **A** tells Larry that he still takes things from the barn.
      ○ **B** says he wouldn't give Larry away to the police even if he had killed someone.
      ○ **C** is so drunk that he falls asleep on Larry's porch.
      ○ **D** demolishes Larry's car with a baseball bat.

    page/line: _____ quote: _____

Analysis

2 a Work with a partner and complete the following sentence.

Wallace Stringfellow is a man who _____ .

   b Compare your sentence with another pair.
   c Work in groups of four and collect at least 10 character adjectives
      to describe Wallace. Find quotes from the text to prove your
      findings.

3 Wallace is definitely not the special friend that Larry's mother used to
   wish for. Explain why.

4 a Look at the following passages. Analyse which techniques Tom
      Franklin uses to characterize Wallace. → Info box, → Language help
      A p. 181, ll. 12–15
      B p. 201, ll. 2–22
      C p. 203, ll. 1–5
      D p. 203, l. 28–p. 204, l. 17

Info Characterization

Characterization is the way in which the author of a fictional text presents his or her
characters to the reader or, in the case of a play or film, to the audience.
There are two main ways of presenting a character:
- **Direct characterization ('telling'):** somebody tells the reader what sort of person
  a character is. This can be:
  - the narrator
  - another character in the story
  - the character him- or herself.
- **Indirect characterization ('showing'):** the reader has to draw conclusions about
  a character based on what the character says and does.

Language help
- … is shown/presented/characterized as somebody who …
- … is characterized by his/her actions/speech, which …

   b Describe the effect of the characterization technique on you,
      the reader.

5 Re-read the passage on p. 206, ll. 27–30. Rephrase it in your own
   words and explain it in the context of chapter 9.
   Consider what it tells you about Larry's sense of belonging.

Beyond the text

6 Work on either **a** or **b**.

a Writing Imagine you had the chance to give Larry some advice on how to continue his relationship with Wallace. Write him a letter taking into account what you found out in tasks 2–4.

b Speaking Imagine you are Larry's mother and you are 'having a good day'. Larry tells you about Wallace. What advice would you give your son on whether or how to continue his relationship with Wallace?

7 In the movie *Into the Wild*, the protagonist Christopher McCandless has chosen to spend some time all by himself in the wilderness of Alaska. Towards the end of this time he reads the famous novel *Dr. Zhivago* by Boris Pasternak and stumbles over this sentence:

'Happiness is only real when shared.'

a Discuss the sentence with reference to *Crooked Letter, Crooked Letter*.

b Go back to your findings from **Module I**, part **B2** (p. 10f.). Discuss how Larry might serve as an example of the connection between belonging and happiness.

8 Writing Choose one of the tasks below.

a Write a poem about being or having a friend.

b Write a poem about Larry and Wallace.

c Write an 'I am ...' poem from Larry's perspective (cf. **Module I, A2**, p. 6).

You may use one of the following skeletons or you may write your own poem.

Diamond poem

Line 1: noun (opposite of line 6)

Line 2: two adjectives about the first noun

Line 3: three verbs about the first noun

Line 4: three verbs about the second noun

Line 5: two adjectives about the second noun

Line 6: noun (opposite of line 1)

Bio poem

Line 1:
contains the name of the character you
want you to think about (Larry/Wallace)

Line 2:
contains three adjectives describing
the person

Line 3:
starts with *Who has loved* …

Line 4:
starts with *Who wanted* …

Line 5:
begins with the word *Always* … and has
the word *never* in it

Line 6:
repeats the name

Making predictions: chapter 10

9 Who says the following quotes in chapter 10?
Write their name in the right column.

*'He wondered how broken Larry was
by the events of his life, how damaged.'*

*'And that was our maid, I can't recall
her name.'*

*'Son, nothing good ever come out
of colors mixing.'*

*'You let him take the blame.
All this time.'*

B10 **Facing the truth** (chapters 10–12)

Comprehension

1 Read chapter 10. Then finish the sentences below and indicate page
and line(s) in the text.

A When Silas tells French how he found Tina Rutherford's body, he _____

_____. (page/line: _____)

B Since Silas wants to stay involved in Larry's case, he offers to _____

_____. (page/line: _____)

C Silas is a bit hesitant about seeing Angie again because he knows that _____

_____. (page/line: _____)

D One night Silas goes into Larry's room and tells him _____

_____. (page/line: _____)

E Silas goes to see Mrs Ott, who tells him that _____

_____. (page/line: _____)

F In a flashback Silas remembers that his mother told him to stop seeing Cindy because

_____. (page/line: _____)

G When Silas tells Angie about his last date with Cindy, Angie _____

_____. (page/line: _____)

H Angie asks Silas what he intends to do once Larry _____

_____. (page/line: _____)

I When Silas feeds Larry's chickens the following day he remembers mowing the grass and

longs to _____

_____. (page/line: _____)

2 Read chapter 11 and correct the mistakes in the text below.
Give page/line references.

Text	Correction	Page/Line
Larry is awake, he remembers dreaming being a boy in the woods. When he wakes up the next time, the doctor tells him that Angie saved his life. French and another police officer interrogate Larry, they ask him why he tried to kill himself. Larry can't remember. When the police officers tell him that Cindy Walker has been found dead in his house, Larry loses consciousness again. When he wakes up, he starts worrying about his mother and asks the nurse to look after her. Larry wants to talk to Wallace and tells the officers that they used to be friends. Then French states clearly that Larry killed Tina Rutherford and that he tried to kill himself later on.		

3 Read chapter 12 and write a three-sentence summary of it.

Analysis

4 a Think: Make a spontaneous decision for yourself and say whether Silas is
- a liar
- a coward or
- a friend.

Take a vote in class and note down the result for each option.

b Pair: Work with a partner and each find two reasons why Silas can be called a liar, a coward or a friend.

c Share: Compare your results with another pair.

5 If you had to describe Silas to someone who has not read the novel, which of the descriptions below would you choose? Why?

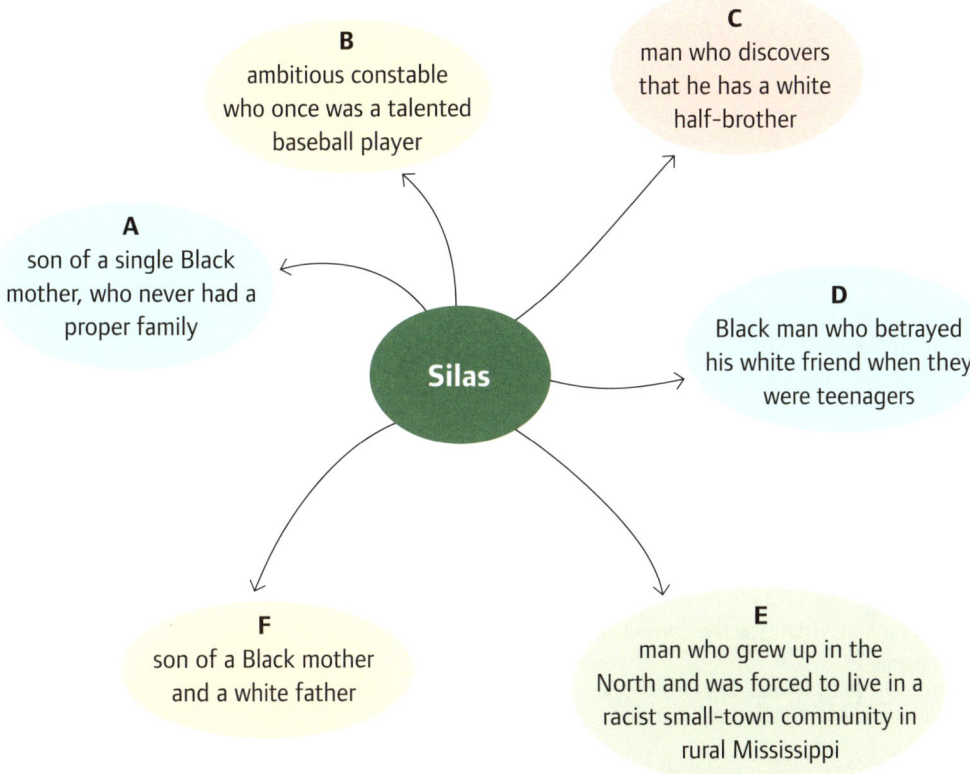

B
ambitious constable who once was a talented baseball player

C
man who discovers that he has a white half-brother

A
son of a single Black mother, who never had a proper family

Silas

D
Black man who betrayed his white friend when they were teenagers

F
son of a Black mother and a white father

E
man who grew up in the North and was forced to live in a racist small-town community in rural Mississippi

6 **Writing** Write a character profile of Silas. Take your findings from tasks **4** and **5** into account and point out
– why he cannot admit his friendship with Larry
– why he lied repeatedly
– why it took him 25 years to come forward with the truth.

Beyond the text

7 Choose one of the following tasks.
a **Speaking** Work with a partner.
– Write a dialogue between Silas and a behavioral therapist he has decided to see. The therapist asks unbiased, neutral questions to find out why Silas has lied so many times and why he can't admit his friendship with Larry.
– Act out your dialogue.
b **Writing** Re-consider everything you have found out about Silas. How do you see him now – friend, liar, coward or something completely different? Write a text in which you explain and substantiate your view. Make sure to explain his sense of belonging.

8 `Listening` 🌐 SPT354924-3 In an interview, Tom Franklin talked about the connections between his life and *Crooked Letter, Crooked Letter*. Listen to the first part of the interview, then mark the following statements as either true or false.

Annotations:
ingratiate yourself with sb.: do things in order to make others like you
invigorate sb.: make sb feel full of energy
strobe (light): bright light that flashes rapidly on and off, used especially at clubs

Statement	True	False
A When writing the novel, Tom Franklin had to rely on his memory.	○	○
B Tom Franklin wanted his main character to be like him because he could identify with him.	○	○
C Tom Franklin tried to become popular as a boy by ingratiating himself with other children.	○	○
D Tom Franklin also had a monster mask like Larry, which he used to make friends.	○	○
E Sometimes objects that Tom Franklin liked as a boy developed their own life in the novel.	○	○

9 `Listening` 🌐 SPT354924-4 Listen to part 2 of the interview with Tom Franklin, then tick the correct option.

Annotations:
contentious: likely to cause disagreement between people
daunting: make sb. feel less confident about sth.

a For *Crooked Letter, Crooked Letter* Tom Franklin had the following idea:

    ○ **A** a mechanic with two brothers
    ○ **B** a Black police officer
    ○ **C** two brothers
    ○ **D** a teacher and a writer

b His friend David Wright told him to …

    ○ **A** make Larry and Silas half brothers.
    ○ **B** have two brothers: one being a police officer and the other a mechanic.
    ○ **C** call the novel *Crooked Letter, Crooked Letter*.
    ○ **D** make Silas a Black policeman.

c Tom Franklin found it challenging to get into the head of a Black character because …

> **A** when you are Black in the USA, you are always aware of being Black.
> **B** he does not know many Black people, only his housekeeper.
> **C** his friend would not give him permission to do it.
> **D** his Black friend did not want to check whether he got things wrong.

Making predictions: chapter 13

10 Make three guesses: what will happen in chapters 13–15?
Note down your ideas and compare them with your partner.

– _____

– _____

– _____

11 Have a look at the hints you collected for **B6**, task **2** (p. 76).
Who might be the man who tried to shoot Larry?

B11 A juncture (chapters 13–15)

Comprehension

1 Read chapters 13–15 and answer the questions below. Make sure to make page/line references:
   a What pieces of evidence does Silas find at Larry's house?
   b What happens at Wallace's house when Silas gets there?
   c What piece of evidence did French find at Wallace's house?

Analysis

2 Re-read p. 259, l. 1 to p. 262, l. 3.
   a Examine the mood Larry is in.
   b Analyse what devices the author employs to create this mood.
3 Re-read p. 280, l. 33 to p. 281, l. 4.
   a Explain the two sentences in the context of the novel.
   b Analyse the stylistic devices used.
4 Explain what effect Silas's confession has, both on himself and on Larry.

Beyond the text

5 a Explain the words *tabloid, yellow press* and *broadsheet* and list the characteristics of the two types of newspapers.

b Choose one of the tasks below.

– **Writing** You are a reporter working for *The Sun Herald*, a local daily tabloid read in Mississippi. Write an article reporting on Larry's case.

– **Writing** You are a reporter working for the *Hattisburg American*, a local daily broadsheet read in Mississippi. Write an article reporting on Larry's case.

c Work with a partner who wrote an article for the other newspaper. Compare your texts and make two lists:
– information covered in both articles
– information only covered in either of your articles.

d Discuss why you chose the information you mentioned in your article. What effect does this have on your readership?

Making predictions: chapter 16

6 Which of the following sentences will you find in chapters 16–19? Explain why you think so.

> **A** 'The land had a way of covering the wrongs of people.'
> **B** 'The land had a way of righting the wrongs of people.'
> **C** 'The land had a way of forgiving the wrongs of people.'

B12 Brothers? (chapters 16–19)

Comprehension

1 Read chapters 16–19 and put the following events in the correct
order. Write the correct numbers in the left column.

_____ **A** Angie comes to visit Silas.

_____ **B** Angie invites Larry to come to church.

_____ **C** French comes to tell Larry and Silas that several pieces of evidence were
found in Wallace's house.

_____ **D** Larry calls a nurse and tells her that he wants to be put into another room.

_____ **E** Larry leaves the hospital and tries to walk back home.

_____ **F** Larry notices that his house has been cleaned and that the rifle
is back in its old place.

_____ **G** Larry offers to repair Silas's car.

_____ **H** Silas and Angie go to Larry's house and put the old rifle back in its place.

_____ **I** Silas gets a phone call, gets into the car and drives Larry home.

_____ **J** Silas leaves and tells Larry that he will come back to visit him.

_____ **K** Silas tells Larry that he found out that they are half-brothers.

_____ **L** Silas tells Larry that, as a child, he wanted to be in his place.

_____ **M** Silas wakes up and finds Larry surfing through the TV channels.

Analysis

2 **a** Are the following characters round or flat (→ Info box)? Tick the
correct box.

Name	Round character	Flat character
Larry	○	○
Silas	○	○
Mr Ott	○	○
Mrs Ott	○	○
Alice Jones	○	○
French	○	○
Angie	○	○

Info Round and flat characters
A **round character** is a character who has
several character traits and behaves in a
life-like way. Usually he or she develops
in the course of the story. The main
characters are usually round characters.
A **flat character** only has a limited number
of character traits and may even just
represent a single quality. Flat characters
are usually minor characters in a novel.

b Discuss results with a partner.

Beyond the text

3 Read the following quote:

> 'He was gone, and I did not have time to tell him what I had just now realized:
> that I forgave him and that she forgave us, and that we had to forgive to survive
> in the labyrinth.'
>
> John Green, Looking for Alaska, Berlin: Cornelsen 2010, p. 217, ll. 7–10

   a Explain the quote in your own words. What might 'the labyrinth'
     stand for?
   b Re-write the quote, replacing some words so that it could occur
     in Crooked Letter, Crooked Letter.

4 **Writing** If you were Larry, would you have forgiven Silas?
Write his monologue, giving reasons why or why not.

5 **Writing** Add one or two page(s) to the novel, starting like this:
One year later ...
Make sure to keep the narrative perspective and keep in mind what
you learned about the characters and their degree of belonging.

6 **Listening** ⊕ SPT354924-5 Listen to part 3 of the interview with
Tom Franklin, then finish the following sentence starters:

   Task 6: annotation
   avalanche: Lawine

   A Tom Franklin knew that he had given the novel a wrong turn when _____

   _____ .

   B He invented Wallace Stringfellow because _____ .

   C Wallace Stringfellow is related to Tom Franklin's own life because _____

   _____ .

7 **Listening** ⊕ SPT354924-6 Listen to part 4 of the interview with
Tom Franklin, then answer the following questions:
   a Which elements in Crooked Letter, Crooked Letter are 'typically
     southern', according to Tom Franklin? Why?
   b Explain why Tom Franklin saw himself as an outsider when he
     was a boy.

Task 7: annotations
(urban) sprawl:
unkontrollierte
Ausbreitung eines
Stadtgebietes
rear (v): (hier) sich
aufbäumen
solipsistic: only being
aware of and thinking
about yourself

8 Franklin says, 'And as the writer I need to identify with all the
characters, even the murderer.' Choose one scene or incident from
the novel and explain the quote.

9 Is Tom Franklin a likeable person to you? Why? Why not?

Part C
Post-reading activities

C1 A book cover

1 Look at the book cover of the novel. Do you find it representative of the story? Why? Why not?
2 Imagine you could make a new book cover for the novel. What would it look like? Describe and explain it to the class. → Language help

> **Language help**
> Kind of picture
> – a black-and-white/color photo of …, a painting/drawing of …
>
> Details
> – background/foreground
> – There is … between / in front of / behind / next to …
> – In the bottom / top right/ left hand corner there is/are …
>
> Effect
> – … makes the observer / potential buyer think of …
> – … touches the observer because …
> – … creates a friendly/romantic/gloomy/spooky/tense atmosphere, which forces the observer to think about …
> – You can feel/anticipate an atmosphere of violence/insecurity/…

C2 A good read?

1 **Writing** Imagine you read *Crooked Letter, Crooked Letter* in your summer holidays. Now you want to tell a friend about it.
Write a book review.

C3 Pictures

1 Bring along a picture (e. g. from old magazines or the internet) that has something to do with the novel, for example with a character, a problem or a scene. The more enigmatic your picture is, the better!
2 Work in groups of four. Each of you shows their picture and the classmates must guess which scene/problem/character in the novel is captured in the picture.
3 Each of you explain why you chose your picture.

C4 A soundtrack

Imagine this novel was turned into a movie.
1 Which scene(s) would you choose for the trailer?
2 What kind of soundtrack would you use for the trailer?
   Describe the music. → Language help

Language help
- The music underlines …
- … creates / should create an atmosphere of … because …
- The music sounds dreamy/spheric/mysterious/powerful/wistful/angry/energetic/ uplifting/eerie/moving/warm/exciting/cheerful/plaintive/monotonous/sad/ rousing/ … because …
- … should make the viewer feel …
- The lyrics support the plot / the conflict / the atmosphere in that …
- The music and the pictures match because …
- instrumental music
- … shows/explains the character's emotions / the setting / the conflict
- … helps build up tension because …

C5 Being a poet

1 **Writing** Fill in the grit to write a haiku (→ Info box) on one of the characters or a situation in the novel.

Info The haiku
The haiku is a three-line poem which usually presents an object in nature and an emotion or a surprising observation that accompanies the perception of that object. It has a very rigid structure (see below).

Line 1:
five syllables

Line 2:
seven to nine syllables

Line 3:
five syllables

C6 Reconsidering things

1 Look again at the pictures in **A1**, task **1** (p. 62). Having read the novel, which picture do you think fits best? Give reasons.
2 Look again at **A7**, task **1** (p. 65) and the text you wrote. Which elements of your text have turned out to be true, which have not?

C7 What sticks in the end …

A review of the novel ends as follows:

'But what sticks at the end is Franklin's shattering, heart-breaking depiction of loneliness.'
From: The Guardian, 4 December 2011

1 Would you agree? Why? Why not?
2 What else 'sticks in the end' for you?

C8 A three-step metaphor

1 Work in groups of three and create three-step metaphors (→ Info box).

Info Three-step metaphors
– **1st round:**
Student A creates a metaphor starting with 'Reading Crooked Letter, Crooked Letter was …'
Student B continues this metaphor with '… because …'
Student C adds the last part starting with '… therefore …'
– **2nd round:**
Student B creates a metaphor starting with 'Reading Crooked Letter, Crooked Letter was …'
Student C continues this metaphor with '… because …'
Student A adds the last part starting with '… therefore …'
– **3rd round**
Student C creates a metaphor starting with 'Reading Crooked Letter, Crooked Letter was …'
Student A continues this metaphor with '… because …'
Student B adds the last part starting with '… therefore …'

Example:
'Reading Crooked Letter, Crooked Letter was a journey to a world yet unknown to me because I met ways of behaving I hadn't encountered before, therefore, it is worthwhile to stand in someone else's shoes now and then.'

2 In your group choose the metaphor you liked best and present it to the class.

The Ambiguity of Belonging – Tying It All Together

Part A
Revisiting *Gran Torino* and *Crooked Letter, Crooked Letter*

A1 Main characters

When working on *Gran Torino* and *Crooked Letter, Crooked Letter* you learned a lot about the protagonists and their sense of belonging.

1 Work in groups of five. Each group member chooses one character from the list below and completes the questionnaire from **Module I**, **D2 (p. 25)** for him or her.
   A Walt
   B Thao
   C Sue
   D Larry
   E Silas
2 Compare and discuss your answers.

A2 Key moments

1 The table below lists situations from the film or the novel in which
the main characters make choices that lead to a new sense of
belonging:

Situation	Choices	Impact
A Walt seeing Sue being harassed at the corner		
B Thao working for Walt		
C Walt and Thao in the barber shop		
D Walt confronting the Hmong gang		
E Larry and Jackie at school		
F Larry fighting with Silas		
G Larry's date with Cindy		
H Wallace visiting Larry		

   a Identify the choices the characters make, analyse their impact and
assess whether the characters succeed at connecting with others
in these particular moments. Make notes.

   b Speaking Form a double circle and discuss each of the situations
above with a different partner.

2 Based on your discussions, add new insights to your questionnaire
from **A1**.

Part B
Exploring identity and belonging: the wider context

B1 Belonging and loneliness

1 Create a collage showing the connections between belonging and loneliness. You could, for example, use photos, illustrations, quotes or song lyrics.

2 `Speaking` Work in pairs. Present your collages to each other and comment on them.

B2 The opposite of loneliness *Marina Keegan*

The author of the article below, Marina Keegan, graduated from Yale University in 2012. The article appeared in a special edition of the Yale University newspaper *The News*. Shortly after the publication, Marina Keegan died tragically in a car accident, aged 22.

We don't have a word for the opposite of loneliness, but if we did, I could say that's what I want in life. What I'm grateful and thankful to have found at Yale, and what I'm scared of losing when we wake up tomorrow and leave this place.

5   It's not quite love and it's not quite community; it's just this feeling that there are people, an abundance of people, who are in this together. Who are on your team. When the check is paid and you stay at the table. When it's four a. m. and no one goes to bed. That night with the guitar. That night we can't remember. That time we did, we went, we
10 saw, we laughed, we felt. The hats.

   Yale is full of tiny circles we pull around ourselves. A cappella groups, sports teams, houses, societies, clubs. These tiny groups that make us feel loved and safe and part of something even on our loneliest nights when we stumble home to our computers – partner-less, tired, awake.
15 We won't have those next year. We won't live on the same block as all our friends. We won't have a bunch of group-texts.

   This scares me. More than finding the right job or city or spouse – I'm scared of losing this web we're in. This elusive, indefinable, opposite of loneliness. This feeling I feel right now.
20   But let us get one thing straight: the best years of our lives are not behind us. They're part of us and they are set for repetition as we grow up and move to New York and away from New York and wish we did or didn't live in New York. I plan on having parties when I'm 30. I plan on having fun when I'm old. Any notion of THE BEST years comes from
25 clichéd 'should haves …', 'if I'd …', 'wish I'd …'

6 abundance: large quantity of sth.
10 hats: reference to the funny-looking hats that Yale graduates traditionally wear at commencement (= graduation) celebrations
12 house: (here) group of students living together in one building and competing with other groups e. g. in sports competitions
18 elusive: difficult to find

Of course, there are things we wished we did: our readings, that boy across the hall. We're our own hardest critics and it's easy to let ourselves down. Sleeping too late. Procrastinating. Cutting corners. More than once I've looked back on my High School self and thought: how did I
30 do that? How did I work so hard? Our private insecurities follow us and will always follow us.

But the thing is, we're all like that. Nobody wakes up when they want to. Nobody did all of their reading (except maybe the crazy people who win the prizes …) We have these impossibly high standards and we'll probably never
35 live up to our perfect fantasies of our future selves. But I feel like that's okay.

We're so young. We're so young. We're twenty-two years old. We have so much time. There's this sentiment I sometimes sense, creeping in our collective conscious as we lay alone after a party, or pack up our books when we give in and go out – that it is somehow too late. That
40 others are somehow ahead. More accomplished, more specialized. More on the path to somehow saving the world, somehow creating or inventing or improving. That it's too late now to BEGIN a beginning and we must settle for continuance, for commencement.

When we came to Yale, there was this sense of possibility. This immense
45 and indefinable potential energy – and it's easy to feel like that's slipped away. We never had to choose and suddenly we've had to. Some of us have focused ourselves. Some of us know exactly what we want and are on the path to get it; already going to med school, working at the perfect NGO, doing research. To you I say both congratulations and you suck.
50 For most of us, however, we're somewhat lost in this sea of liberal arts. Not quite sure what road we're on and whether we should have taken it. If only I had majored in biology … if only I'd gotten involved in journalism as a freshman … if only I'd thought to apply for this or for that …

What we have to remember is that we can still do anything. We can
55 change our minds. We can start over. Get a post-bac or try writing for the first time. The notion that it's too late to do anything is comical. It's hilarious. We're graduating college. We're so young. We can't, we MUST not lose this sense of possibility because in the end, it's all we have.

In the heart of a winter Friday night my freshman year, I was dazed
60 and confused when I got a call from my friends to meet them at EST EST EST. Dazedly and confusedly, I began trudging to SSS, probably the point on campus farthest away. Remarkably, it wasn't until I arrived at the door that I questioned how and why exactly my friends were partying in Yale's administrative building. Of course, they weren't. But it was cold and
65 my ID somehow worked so I went inside SSS to pull out my phone. It was quiet, the old wood creaking and the snow barely visible outside the stained glass. And I sat down. And I looked up. At this giant room I was in. At this place where thousands of people had sat before me. And alone, at night, in the middle of a New Haven storm, I felt so remarkably,
70 unbelievably safe.

28 procrastinate: delay doing something because you do not want to do it
28 cut corners: do sth. the easiest way
38 collective conscious: kollektives Bewusstsein
48 med school = medical school
49 NGO = non-governmental organization
49 suck: (sl) be very bad
50 liberal arts: Geisteswissenschaften
52 major in sth.: choose sth. as main subject of study at university
53 freshman: college student in the first year
55 post-bac: after receiving a Bachelor's degree
57 hilarious: extremely funny, ridiculous
60–61 EST EST EST: Italian restaurant in New Haven
61 SSS (= Sheffield-Sterling-Strathcona Hall): large building on the campus of Yale university which includes an auditorium and seminar rooms

We don't have a word for the opposite of loneliness, but if we did, I'd say that's how I feel at Yale. How I feel right now. Here. With all of you. In love, impressed, humbled, scared. And we don't have to lose that.

We're in this together, 2012. Let's make something happen to this world.

From: Yale Daily News, *27 May 2012*

73 humbled: not proud or arrogant

Comprehension

1 What is 'the opposite of loneliness' according to Marina Keegan? List the answers she gives in her article.

Analysis

2 Compare Marina Keegan's ideas about 'the opposite of loneliness' to your own ideas from **B1**.

3 Use the concept of the ambiguity of belonging to analyse and explain Marina Keegan's feelings and her coping strategies.

Language help
- a strong/deep/intense/distinct/nagging/vague feeling about sth.
- appear/feel/become/remain optimistic/pessimistic about sth.
- arouse/evoke a strong feeling of …
- be left with / be given the feeling that …
- feel ambiguous/uncertain/uncomfortable/uneasy about sth.
- have mixed feelings about sth.
- have a tight feeling in your stomach
- show optimism/resilience/strength

Beyond the text

4 Trace Walt, Thao, Larry and Silas's 'roads to belonging'. The following questions may help you:
- Which roads have the four characters taken?
- Where have they lost their way?
- Where have they started all over?
- Have they found a 'sense of possibility' (cf. l. 44) in their lives?

B3 Belonging and diversity

In **B2**, Marina Keegan writes about 'tiny circles' (l. 11) that contribute to her sense of belonging.

1 **Think:** Write a short text explaining the connection between *belonging* and *fitting in*.

2 **Pair:** Compare your answers with a partner.

3 **Share:** Discuss whether culturally diverse societies like ours place too much emphasis on fitting in today.

B4 Overcoming differences *William Shakespeare*

In May 1517, during the reign of King Henry VIII, a riot against foreigners broke out in London. Around 1600, William Shakespeare turned this incident into a dramatic scene. In the following excerpt, Thomas More, then deputy sheriff, is addressing the rioters, appealing to them to change their minds about London's immigrants.

William Shakespeare (1564–1616)

Grant them removed, and grant that this your noise
Hath chid down all the majesty of England;
Imagine that you see the wretched strangers,
Their babies at their backs and their poor luggage,
5 Plodding to th'ports and coasts for transportation,
And that you sit as kings in your desires,
Authority quite silent by your brawl,
And you in ruff of your opinions clothed;
What had you got? I'll tell you: you had taught
10 How insolence and strong hand should prevail,
How order should be quelled; and by this pattern
Not one of you should live an aged man,
For other ruffians, as their fancies wrought,
With self same hand, self reasons, and self right,
15 Would shark on you, and men like ravenous fishes
Would feed on one another …

Say now the king,
As he is clement, if th'offender mourn,
Should so much come too short of your great trespass
20 As but to banish you, whither would you go?
What country, by the nature of your error,
Should give you harbour? Go you to France or Flanders,
To any German province, to Spain or Portugal,
Nay, any where that not adheres to England,
25 Why, you must needs be strangers: would you be pleased
To find a nation of such barbarous temper,
That, breaking out in hideous violence,
Would not afford you an abode on earth,
Whet their detested knives against your throats,
30 Spurn you like dogs, and like as if that God
Owed not nor made not you, nor that the claimants
Were not all appropriate to your comforts,
But chartered unto them? What would you think
To be thus used? this is the strangers case;
35 And this your mountainish inhumanity.

From: The Booke of Sir Thomas Moore, *1601–1604*

1 grant: (here) suppose
2 hath … England: has shouted down England's greatness
3 wretched: in poor condition
6 as kings in your desires: ruled by passion, not by thought
7 authority: government
7 brawl: (here) noise
8 in ruff … clothed: self-righteously, arrogantly
10 insolence: very rude behaviour
11 quell sth.: stop sth.
13 ruffian: criminal
13 as their fancies wrought: as they pleased
14 self same: exactly the same
15 shark on sb.: attack sb.
15 ravenous: very hungry
18 clement: showing kindness
19 mourn: (here) regret your behavior
20 whither: where
24 that not adheres to sth.: that is not part of sth.
25 needs: necessarily
28 afford sb. sth.: offer sb. sth.
28 abode: shelter
29 whet sth.: (here) put/place sth.
30 spurn sb.: beat sb. up
31 claimants: (here) what others own
32 appropriate to your comforts: good enough for you:
33 but chartered unto them: only meant to be used by them

Statue of Sir Thomas More (1478–1535) at Chelsea Old Church, London

Comprehension

1 In the table below, match the parts of Thomas More's speech on the left to the headings on the right by writing the correct letter in the middle. There are two more headings than parts.

Part I: ll. 1–7	_____	**A** Injustice beyond compare
		B The immigrants' reactions
Part II: ll. 8–16	_____	**C** The king's views
		D Violence begets violence
Part III: ll. 17–33	_____	**E** What if the rioters were successful?
		F What if the same happened to the rioters?
Part IV: ll. 34–35	_____	

2 Sum up Thomas More's message to the rioters in one sentence.

_____

_____

Analysis

3 Analyse Shakespeare's use of stylistic devices to describe the rioters and their attitudes.

> **Info Stylistic devices**
> In stylistic devices, words are used beyond their literal meanings to create a special effect. Commonly used stylistic devices are:
> – simile: direct comparison using *like* or *as*
> – metaphor: indirect comparison without *like* or *as*
> – allusion: direct or indirect reference to sb. or sth. the reader is supposed to recognize
> – contrast: opposing views, words or characters brought together for emphasis
> – symbol: thing, word or phrase standing for an abstract idea
> – personification: presentation of animals or objects as if they were human beings

Beyond the text

4   Relate the concept of the ambiguity of belonging to the situation of
   people leaving war-torn or impoverished countries to seek refuge
   elsewhere. → Language help

> **Language help**
> – influx/flow/plight/return of refugees/migrants
> – house/accept/resettle/expel/return / take in refugees
> – a(n) genuine/economic/environmental/war/political refugee
> – be forced to flee
> – try/manage to flee
> – be recognized / qualify as a refugee
> – flee empty-handed / in panic/terror
> – flee from persecution / to safety
> – make Germany/Europe/America/ … your new home
> – migrate from/to (a country)
> – suffer badly/greatly/severely/terribly/needlessly
> – seek/apply for political asylum
> – be persecuted for religious/political reasons

5   Discuss how relevant Shakespeare's message is today.

B5 Belonging to the global community

1   Martin Luther King, in a sermon on world peace delivered on Christ-
   mas Eve in 1967, reminded his audience of the following:

> *'Before you finish eating breakfast this morning,*
> *you've depended on more than half the world.'*
>
> Martin Luther King

Explain Martin Luther King's words.

A bust of Martin Luther King (1929-1968)

2 The newspaper headlines below highlight different ways in which people are connected around the world today.

'I am a Global Citizen' – Global Citizen initiative holds conference in Rome.

Hongkong, Austria or New Zealand?
Now's the time to consider a university abroad

Cultural convergence: will we all become Americanized?

NY, Rio, Tokyo:
What's 'heimat' in a globalized world?

Transnational corporations about to take over nation-states as world leaders

New Zealand company lays off workers – cheaper production in Indonesia

Super Bowl 50 draws more than 110 million viewers worldwide

Third culture kids – soon to be the norm?

Starbucks to open first store in Vietnam

Earth Day events planned in 193 countries

a Work in groups of four. Take turns choosing a headline and explaining what it tells you about interconnectedness between people.

b Speaking In your group discuss why developing a global sense of belonging is important in an interconnected world. Agree on a group statement and present it in class.

Part C
Wrapping up

C1 Self-assessment

1 Write down …
   a three important ideas related to the concept *ambiguity of belonging*.
   b two examples each from *Gran Torino* and *Crooked Letter, Crooked Letter* illustrating your ideas.
   c one question you still have.
2 Compare your answers with a partner.

C2 Culminating task

1 Writing Imagine you are nearing graduation and you have decided to write an article for your Abitur paper about belonging being a personal and a global challenge for your generation.
   Write your article, referring to your own experiences and the various aspects of belonging you discussed in the previous modules. Choose one of the quotes below as the beginning of your piece or find one yourself.

> 'The wise man belongs to all countries, for the home of a great soul is the whole world.'
> Democritus

> 'As we grow in awareness of one another – whether two people beginning a romance or two disparate and far-removed strangers taking an interest in the other's culture – a wonderful thing begins to happen: we begin to care for the other as if the other is part of us.'
> Scott A. Hunt

> 'We may have all come on different ships, but we're in the same boat now.'
> Martin Luther King

> 'This above all: to thine own self be true. And it must follow as the night the day, Thou canst not then be false to any man.'
> William Shakespeare, Hamlet (Act I, Scene 3)

Talking about Core Concepts

A1 Focusing on language

Work on your own.

Tips
Use a collocation dictionary to complete the tasks.
Choose word combinations that are helpful to talk and write about *Gran Torino* and *Crooked Letter, Crooked Letter*.

1 Write the correct preposition in the gap:

A integrate sb. _____ a group

B feel alienated _____ society

C be prejudiced _____ other customs and cultures

D discriminate _____ immigrants

E feel estranged _____ sb.

2 Cross out the verb that does NOT collocate with the given noun phrase:

A assume/change/develop/consult   + one's identity
B display/exhibit/agree/show   + macho behavior
C emphasize/do/reflect/perceive   + cultural differences
D deny/prove/refute/speak   + allegations
E demand/take/pay/swear   + vengeance
F inflict/submit/suffer/show   + cruelty

3 Find at least four verbs collocating with the given nouns.

A _____ / _____ / _____ / _____ a relationship with sb.

B _____ / _____ / _____ / _____ expectations

C _____ / _____ / _____ / _____ responsibility

D _____ / _____ / _____ / _____ a sense of belonging

E _____ / _____ / _____ / _____ choices

4 Find at least four suitable adjectives collocating with the given nouns.

A a(n) _____ / _____ / _____ / _____ language

B a(n) _____ / _____ / _____ / _____ friendship

C a(n) _____ / _____ / _____ / _____ community

D a(n) _____ / _____ / _____ / _____ culture

E a(n) _____ / _____ / _____ / _____ choice

5 Combine words from box 1 with words from box 2 to form as many compound nouns as possible.

Box 1	Box 2
peer · male · macho · language · gang · family	barriers · behavior · bonding · culture · pressure · relations

6 Form meaningful word combinations using the following words:

values · family · feelings · bonds · relationship · issue · alienation · challenges · pressure · self-esteem · circle · sacrifices · ritual · tensions · relations · friendship · share · dysfunctional · ambiguous · social · strained · gender · fail to · face · peer · growing · vicious · make · fit in · initiation · race · interracial

A2 Using language in context

Work with a partner.

1 Explain which role the concepts in the box below play for characters in *Gran Torino* and *Crooked Letter, Crooked Letter*, e. g. 'Larry is not integrated into the school community, which is shown when …'. Use the word combinations you have formed in **A1**.

choice	language	friendship	relationships	responsibility
culture	alienation	acceptance	expectations	sense of belonging
prejudice	integration	community	discrimination	loneliness

2 Talk about the main characters in *Gran Torino* and *Crooked Letter, Crooked Letter* by forming complex sentences, using the word combinations you have formed in **A1** and words in the box below:

Conjunctions	Linking words	Adverbs
if · but · when · while · because · although · so (that)	nevertheless · however · as a result · as a consequence · in fact · in particular · on the other hand	unfortunately · obviously · hardly · clearly · sadly · apparently · undoubtedly

Acknowledgements

Texts:

p. 7: Sylvia Loh, unveröffentliches Gedicht. Mit freundlicher Genehmigung der Autorin; **p. 9:** *From Why Are All the Black Kids Sitting Together in the Cafeteria: And Other Conversations About Race* by Beverly Daniel Tatum, copyright © 1997. Reprinted by permission of Basic Books, an imprint of Perseus Books, LLC, a subsidiary of Hachette Book Group, Inc.; **p. 11:** Blake Lively, What's The Secret To Happiness, Copyright The Telegraph 2016; **p 13:** Fixing America's inner cities, copyright The Economist 2017; **p. 20:** Katrin Zeug, Longing For Acceptance /Süchtig nach Anerkennung Copyright *Zeit online* 2013; **p. 21:** Ndéla Faye, Am I Rootless, Or Am I Free? Copyright *Guardian News & Media Ltd* 2017; **p. 39–42:** Nick Schenk, Zitate aus dem Screenplay "Gran Torino"; **p. 44:** Matern Boeselager, Mit dem Baseballschläger gegen Nazis, *www.vice.com;* **p. 47:** Nick Schenk, Zitate aus dem Screenplay "Gran Torino"; **p. 50:** "Gran Torino's Hmong Lead Bee Vang on Film, Race, and Masculinity: Conversations with Louisa Schein" *Hmong Studies Journal*, Volume li: l-11, Spring 2010 httn:/Ihmonstudies.org/ ScheinVangRSJ1 I .pdf; **p. 53:** Nick Schenk, Zitate aus dem Screenplay "Gran Torino"; **p. 56:** Werk: Gran Torino /Text: Cullum, James / Eastwood, Clint / Eastwood, Kyle / Stevens, Michael Christopher / Copyright: Cibie Music / EMI Music Publishing Ltd / Robie Springs Music / Upward and onward / Wallet Music / Warner Olive Music LLC / Warner-Barham Music LLC / Neue Welt Musikverlag GmbH, Hamburg / EMI Music Publishing Germany GmbH, Berlin / Universal Music Publishing GmbH, Berlin; **p. 58:** Peter Bradshaw, Gran Torino, Copyright *Guardian News & Media* Ltd 2017; **p. 65:** Auszüge aus dem Roman *Crooked Letter, Crooked Letter* von Tom Franklin, mit freundlicher Genehmigung des Autors, Veröffentlicht mit Genehmigung Nr. 71 378 der Paul & Fritz AG in Zürich; **p. 77:** Nikolas Piper, Revolution ohne Anführer Copyright *Süddeutsche Zeitung* 2017; **p. 88:** Auszüge aus dem Roman *Crooked Letter, Crooked Letter* von Tom Franklin, mit freundlicher Genehmigung des Autors, Veröffentlicht mit Genehmigung Nr. 71 378 der Paul & Fritz AG in Zürich; **p. 102:** From THE OPPOSITE OF LONELINESS by Marina Keegan. Copyright © 2014 by Tracy and Kevin Keegan. Reprinted with the permission of Scribner, a division of Simon & Schuster, Inc. All rights reserved.

Audiotexts:

p. 71/73: ©2016 National Public Radio, Inc. NPR news report titled "Why Busing Didn't End School Segregation"; **p. 92, 96:** With kind permission of Tom Franklin

Photos/Illustrations:

Cover: picture alliance / moodboard; **p. 6:** picture alliance / moodboard; **p. 7:** Fotolia/ © mshch; **p. 10:** Fotolia/© Viacheslav Iakobchuk; **p. 12:** With kind permission of Harvard Business Publishing; **p. 14:** Fotolia/© jonbilous; **p. 18:** picture alliance / moodboard; **p. 19:** bpk / The Art Institute of Chicago / Art Resource, NY; **p. 20:** imago/Metodi Popow; **p. 21:** top – © 2000–2006 Adobe Systems; bottom – Shutterstock / Lukasz Stefanski; **p. 23:** Ungermeyer; **p. 26:** mauritius images / Performance Image / Alamy; **p. 34:** GRAN TORINO, Clint Eastwood, 2008. ©Warner Bros./Courtesy; **p. 35:** Shutterstock / Robert Hoetink; **p. 39:** left + right – Copyright ©Warner Bros/courtesy Everett Collection / Everett Collection; **p. 42:** Fotolia/© efired; **p. 43:** Fotolia/© EdwardSamuel; **p. 44:** Shutterstock / Axente Vlad; **p. 48:** Copyright © Warner Bros/courtesy Everett Collection / Everett Collection; **p. 50:** Fotolia/© Christian Frisell; **p. 52:** Shutterstock / Thampitakkull Jakkree; **p. 54:** Fotolia/© Vadimsadovski; **p. 57:** Fotolia/© lassedesignen; **p. 60:** action press/ Sundholm, Magnusaction press; **p. 62** top half: © Alfred Buellesbach /VISUM creative; **p. 62** bottom half: top left – Fotolia/© anadman22; top center – Fotolia/© jdoms; top right – Shutterstock / David Lee; middle left – Fotolia/© franz12; middle center Fotolia/ © peshkova; middle right – Fotolia/© Fotoluminate LLC; bottom left – Shutterstock / serpeblu; bottom center – Fotolia/© Bits and Splits; bottom right – Fotolia/© komokvm; **p. 67:** Shutterstock / Costea Andrea M; **p. 69:** top left – Fotolia/ © Shane; top right – Colourbox /Jose Manuel Gelpi Diaz; bottom left – Shutterstock / Johnny Adolphson; bottom right – Colourbox.com **p. 78:** INTERFOTO / SuperStock; **p. 83:** Christian Heeb/laif; **p. 94:** Fotolia/© Pierre-Jean DURIEU **p. 100:** picture alliance / moodboard; **p. 105:** Shutter-stock/ Stocksnapper; **p. 106:** Fotolia/ Pauws99@Yahoo.co.uk; **p. 107:** Shutterstock/ fotomak